INTRODUCING

Marquis de
Sade

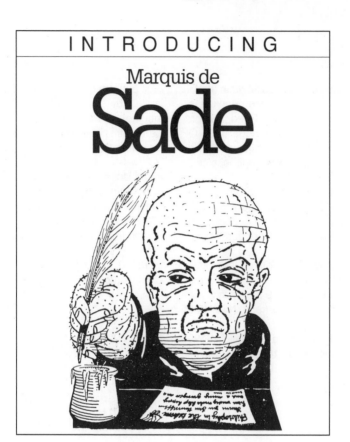

Stuart Hood and Graham Crowley

Edited by Richard Appignanesi

ICON BOOKS UK   TOTEM BOOKS USA

This edition published in the UK
in 1999 by Icon Books Ltd.,
Grange Road, Duxford,
Cambridge CB2 4QF
email: icon@mistral.co.uk
www.iconbooks.co.uk

Distributed in the UK, Europe,
Canada, South Africa and Asia by the
Penguin Group: Penguin Books Ltd.,
27 Wrights Lane, London W8 5TZ

This edition published in Australia
in 1999 by Allen & Unwin Pty. Ltd.,
PO Box 8500, 9 Atchison Street,
St. Leonards NSW 2065

Previously published in the UK in 1995
and Australia in 1996 under the title
Marquis de Sade for Beginners

First published in the United States
in 1999 by Totem Books
Inquiries to: PO Box 223,
Canal Street Station,
New York, NY 10013

In the United States,
distributed to the trade by
National Book Network Inc.,
4720 Boston Way, Lanham,
Maryland 20706

Library of Congress Catalog
Card Number: 99–071125

Originating editor: Richard Appignanesi

Printed and bound in Australia
by McPherson's Printing Group, Victoria

PC 25 b 22.

This the shelf-mark in the British Library for **Juliette**, a novel by the Marquis de Sade.

The shelf-mark indicates that the book is considered to belong to a "special category". When you have been issued with the book, you will not be allowed to sit and read it where you please but will be assigned to a seat under the eyes of the library staff. Clearly, what you have in your hands is dangerous stuff! Never mind that his works can be bought in perfectly respectable bookshops or that they have been the subject of serious critical discussion.

In placing Sade's works in a special category, the British Library is perpetuating a tradition which has lasted for more than a hundred years of dismissing his work as mere pornography. The British Library is not alone in its attitude, for the **Encyclopedia Britannica** (1911 edition) begins a remarkably short entry by describing him as "a licentious French writer". And yet, great literary figures, philosophers and scholars in Europe and elsewhere have paid tribute to Sade's importance as a libertarian thinker, and, indeed, a moralist. What is the truth about Sade?

Sade's Origins

Donatien-Alphonse-François, Marquis de Sade, was descended from medieval Provençal nobility of Italian origin. No portrait of Sade survives, but several contemporary descriptions of him, including a police warrant of 1793, agree in the details.

He was blonde, blue-eyed, rather short, chubby and considered attractive.

Libertines

His father, Jean-Baptiste-Joseph-François, Comte de Sade, was a member of the "nobility of the sword" and lord of several manors, notably the château of La Coste in the Lubéron mountains east of Avignon. The Comte de Sade served all his life in the army and diplomatic service. His wife Marie-Éléonore was related to the royal house of Bourbon.

Sade's father, a dedicated libertine who enjoyed equally his many mistresses and young male prostitutes, wrote verses expressing a preference for anal intercourse with women. Sade carefully preserved his father's writings. His mother retired to a Carmelite convent in Paris, rue de l'Enfer, around 1760.

From 1745 to 1750, Sade passed to the care of his uncle, Jacques-François-Paul-Aldonse, Abbé de Sade, a Vicar-General and abbot. The Abbé de Sade was a friend of the free-thinking philosopher Voltaire and a notorious libertine, briefly jailed in 1762 for debauchery. He lived openly with two mistresses, a mother and daughter.

Gloomy Castles

Sade's years with his uncle in the family château of Saumane and the abbey of Ébreuil impressed him with memories of gloomy battlements and deep dungeons.

The Abbé de Sade, a biographer of the great Italian scholar and poet Petrarch (1304–74), was obsessed by a Provençal legend.

Laura, the legendary muse, would later become a comfort to Sade in his Vincennes prison, as we shall see.

The Jesuit Theatre

Sade's formal education only lasted four years and took place at the aristocratic Lycée Louis-le-Grand in Paris run by Jesuits. Here he received a traditional grounding in the classics. The Jesuits were educational innovators who encouraged theatrical experiments.

Sade's passion for the theatre endured all his life.

The Jesuits also believed in the efficacy of corporal punishment.

If Sade was obsessively addicted to anal-eroticism, both in practice and in his imaginative writing, it is likely to have had its roots in his experiences under the rod of the Fathers in an institution where homosexuality was also common.

The Cavalry Officer

At the age of 14, Sade entered the cavalry training school of the King's Light Horse Regiment and, as a member of the nobility, automatically became a second lieutenant. He saw active service in the Netherlands during the Seven Years' War (1756–63).

I AM SURE I GAVE A GOOD ACCOUNT OF MYSELF. THE NATURAL IMPETUOSITY OF MY CHARACTER, THAT FIERY SOUL WITH WHICH NATURE ENDOWED ME, SERVED TO ENHANCE THAT UNFLINCHING SAVAGERY MEN CALL COURAGE.

Sade spent 17 years in the army, ending up a cavalry captain and maître de camp. In 1764, he acquired from his father the post of lieutenant general of four provinces: Bresse, Bugey, Valromey and Gex.

The Apprentice Libertine

Sade in his early twenties already had a "wild" reputation for debauchery, heavy debts and impatience with army discipline. Sade has left us what seems a frank self-portrait.

"Related through my mother to the greatest families in the realm, attached on my father's side to everyone of distinction in the province of Languedoc; born in Paris in the lap of luxury and plenty, I thought as soon as I could think that nature and fortune had combined to heap their gifts on me; I thought so because people were silly enough to tell me so and this ridiculous prejudice made me haughty, despotic and irascible; it seemed that everyone should yield to me, that the entire universe should flatter my whims, and that I alone possessed the right to conceive and satisfy such whims."

Marriage

The Comte de Sade, worried about his spoilt, libertine son, arranged a marriage for him in 1763 with Renée-Pélagie de Montreuil from the "nobility of the robe" which furnished France with her judges, lawyers and administrators.

Renée's father was President of the Court of Taxation and very rich, being what Sade called a "tax extortioner" responsible for collecting revenue.

Signing the marriage contract was delayed to allow Sade to recover from a gonorrhoeal infection.

Laure came from the same Provençal nobility as himself and Sade considered himself engaged to her. He was deeply disappointed at having to renounce her but was fortunate in the wife chosen for him. She would prove constantly supportive through many difficult years.

First Imprisonment

Five months after the wedding, Jeanne Testard, a young fan-maker, complained to the police about Sade's excesses.

Testard claimed to have refused both flagellation and anal intercourse (a capital crime at the time). The blasphemies were allegedly Sade's desecration of a chalice, profanation of the names of Jesus and the Virgin Mary and boasts of defiling Communion wafers by inserting them in a woman's vagina: serious crimes which earned Sade his first taste of prison, two weeks in the Vincennes fortress on the King's command.

The Vice Inspector

His mother-in-law, Madame de Montreuil, tried to buy Testard's silence. He was released into the Montreuils' custody at the Château d'Echauffour. Sade was now under the constant observation of Inspector Marais, head of the Paris vice squad.

Inspector Marais reported straight to the King on the precise details of the sexual behaviour of Sade and other aristocrats.

LIKE OTHER YOUNG MEN OF HIS CLASS, THE MARQUIS HANGS ABOUT STAGE-DOORS, NO DOUBT DUE TO HIS INTEREST IN THE THEATRE, BUT ALSO BECAUSE IT IS EXCELLENT HUNTING-GROUND FOR RICH MEN LOOKING FOR ACTRESSES AND DANCERS TO EXPLOIT...

WITH ONE ACTRESS CALLED MLLE BEAUVOISIN, WHOSE CLIENTS INCLUDE OTHER ARISTOCRATS, HE HAS A PARTICULAR LIAISON.

MLLE BEAUVOISIN ACCOMPANIED HIM SOUTH TO THE FAMILY CASTLE AT LA COSTE WHERE HE PRESENTED HER AS HIS WIFE.

SHE TOOK PART IN THE PERFORMANCES ON THE STAGE HE HAD BUILT AT LA COSTE, HIS MOTHER-IN-LAW WAS NATURALLY ANNOYED.

OF COURSE I'M ANNOYED THIS CAN'T GO ON. SOMETHING MUST BE DONE TO RESTRAIN THE MARQUIS.

The pattern was set for a course of enmity between Sade and Mme de Montreuil that would soon lead her to have him put away.

The Rose Keller Affair

On Easter Sunday, 1768 (note the day!) Sade picked up Rose Keller, a 36-year-old widow begging in Place des Victoires. On the pretext of hiring Keller as a chambermaid, he took her to a house in the Paris suburb of Arcueil where a couple of prostitutes were already installed.

Afterwards, Sade tended her wounds, fed her and locked her up. But she escaped and reported her experience to some village women who took her to the police.

Mme de Montreuil once again saw to it that Rose Keller was bribed to keep silent. But the case passed from the local magistrature to a higher criminal court which declared Sade under arrest.

A **lettre de cachet**, bearing the King's seal and ordering the imprisonment without trial of the person named in it, was commonly used to confine those whose conduct was likely to bring discredit to their families. And so, Sade was duly imprisoned, which removed him from court jurisdiction and thus, it was hoped, avoiding public scandal.

A Public Outcry

Too late! The Keller affair had caused widespread indignation. A woman friend writing to the Abbé de Sade described the prevailing mood.

"Public hatred is aroused against him beyond all description. Judge of it yourself. People think he indulged in this insane flagellation in order to mock the Passion. He is a victim of the public's ferocity."

The case went to the high-level criminal court of La Tournelle. Sade admitted the whipping but disputed its severity and Keller's details.

SHE KNEW EXACTLY WHAT I WAS HIRING HER FOR... I DIDN'T TIE HER DOWN AND ONLY WHIPPED HER THREE OR FOUR TIMES WITH KNOTTED CORDS. I DIDN'T CUT HER BUT MERELY SMEARED A LITTLE WHITE-WAX SALVE ON HER BROKEN SKIN...

Sade got off with a trifling fine. He was released and ordered by the King to remain in exile at La Coste. That winter in remote La Coste, Sade put on a comedy he had written himself in the château's theatre.

1772: the Marseilles Affair

The next crisis occurred in Marseilles at an orgy including four young girls procured by Sade's valet, Armand Latour. The usual whippings, masturbation and sodomy took place with Latour playing an active part.

The sweets made two girls ill and poisoning was suspected.

The case went to the Seneschal's Court of Marseilles and the Royal Prosecutor issued warrants for the arrest of Sade and his valet.

Anne-Prospère de Launay, a guest at La Coste, was a lay canoness who lived in a convent but had taken no vows. Together they travelled to Italy where Mlle de Launay posed as Sade's wife.

In their absence, the Marseilles court sentenced Sade to beheading for poisoning and sodomy and Latour to hanging, their bodies to be burned and their ashes scattered. The sentence was duly carried out with effigies of Sade and Latour on 12 September 1772 in the Place des Prêcheurs at Aix. Sade's reaction to this was one of contempt for the judges. "The brave Marquis de S***, when informed of the magistrates' decision to burn him in effigy, pulled out his prick and exclaimed . . . "

Imprisoned in the Kingdom of Sardinia

Sade's elopement with his sister-in-law was technically incest. This scandalous affront to family honour was too much for Mme de Montreuil. Fearful of being arrested once more, Sade settled down just over the border from France in Chambéry, which was then in the Kingdom of Sardinia. On learning this, Mme de Montreuil through the French ambassador requested the King of Sardinia to imprison the Marquis.

Sade was jailed in another fortress, Miolans, situated in the mountains not far from Chambéry, which prefigured the isolated castles of his later fiction. He was in effect his mother-in-law's prisoner. Meanwhile, oddly enough, his sister-in-law had gone back to La Coste.

Escape

His wife Renée instead made her way to Miolans in men's clothing in an unsuccessful attempt to gain her husband's release.

BUT WITH MY DEAR RENÉE'S HELP I ESCAPED AND RETURNED TO FRANCE.

RENÉE

Mme de Montreuil obtained another order to have Sade imprisoned, but he eluded the police and took refuge in his La Coste château. Here he spent the winter of 1774 with Renée, a remarkable and long-suffering woman who constantly proved herself supportive.

Another Scandal at La Coste

That winter at La Coste, Sade hired five girls and a young male secretary who took part in orgies. Renée herself might have been involved.

The parents of some of the young women then alleged that they had been abducted and criminal proceedings were started against the Marquis. With the support of her mother, who was as always anxious to stifle scandal, Renée saw to it that the young women were spirited away, hidden or otherwise silenced.

Travels in Italy

Sade himself set off for Italy where he travelled extensively. He would later draw on his travels to write an account of his **Voyage d'Italie**. More importantly his itinerary through Turin and Florence to Rome and Naples, meeting persons of the highest rank, would be followed by one of his most famous creations – the heroine of his long novel **Juliette**.

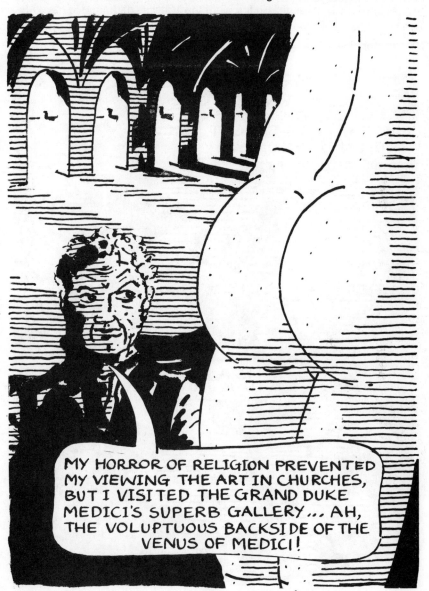

MY HORROR OF RELIGION PREVENTED MY VIEWING THE ART IN CHURCHES, BUT I VISITED THE GRAND DUKE MEDICI'S SUPERB GALLERY... AH, THE VOLUPTUOUS BACKSIDE OF THE VENUS OF MEDICI!

The "Justine" Incident

In 1776, Sade was back in La Coste. He required a cook and a Franciscan friar, Father Durand, obligingly hired a pretty girl for him. Sade called her "Justine", a name he would make famous as the heroine of another novel and sister to Juliette. Four more servants were hired. The morning after their arrival, they all left except "Justine" and reported to her father, a weaver, that in the night the Marquis had "tried to have his way with them by offering a purse of silver". The weaver stormed up to castle with a pistol.

Before the Courts Again

Sade then went to Paris with Renée and "Justine" who begged to be taken with them. In Paris he was arrested by Inspector Marais of the vice squad and returned to the fortress of Vincennes.

In 1778, escorted by Marais, he appeared once more before the High Courts of Aix and Marseilles to face revised charges connected with the 1772 affair.

Sade was still a prisoner by virtue of Mme de Montreuil's royal **lettre de cachet**. On his way back to Vincennes, he escaped from the custody of Marais and fled to La Coste.

Prison Without End . . .

In August 1778, he was apprehended at La Coste by Inspector Marais.

So began 10 years of imprisonment, first at Vincennes and then in the Paris Bastille.

What Is a Pervert?

Sade favoured anal intercourse with women but was himself addicted to anal penetration by others. To obtain sexual satisfaction in his long years in prison, he resorted to instruments provided by his understanding wife who had them manufactured to order.

Freud remarks that "no healthy person . . . can fail to make some addition that might be called perverse to the normal sexual aim."

That Sade's sexual formation was in this sense an example of "perversion" is clear but his recorded behaviour is no more aberrant than that of the numerous males who today – as then – obtain sexual satisfaction from the "hum and bond" advertised in the telephone kiosks of our great cities.

Anal Obsession

The element remarkable in Sade's life and fictions is **coprophilia** – a fascination with excrement and bodily smells, which may extend to **coprophagy**, eating or licking excrement.

Freud warns us that even here we should not assume that such people are insane. Sade was certainly anally obsessed and in his fantasies he carried anal eroticism to the limits, but he was definitely not insane.

THIS ILLUSTRATES THE ASTONISHING LENGTHS TO WHICH PEOPLE WILL GO IN SUCCESSFULLY OVERRIDING THE RESISTANCES OF SHAME, DISGUST, HORROR OR PAIN ... TO ACHIEVE PLEASURE.

The Bad Prisoner in Cell No. 6

Sade was anything but a model prisoner. The commandant of the Miolans fortress in Savoy, from which Sade had escaped, described him "as unreliable as he is hot-tempered and impulsive and capable of some desperate action". Writing to Renée in 1783, Sade characterized himself as . . .

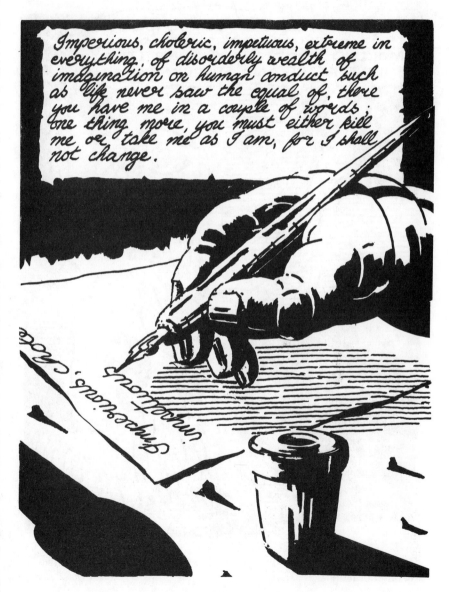

37

Monsieur No. 6

Sade's time in Vincennes as "Monsieur No. 6" (the number of his cell) began with three months' solitary confinement. Eventually cell no. 6 became reasonably furnished and he was able, thanks to Renée, to pay for a sumptuous diet.

This rich diet combined with inadequate exercise led to extreme obesity and deterioration.

Sade complained bitterly of the restrictions on the time he was allowed to exercise outside his cell. In two months, he wrote to Renée, he had been permitted five walks of one hour each in a sort of tomb 40 feet square surrounded by walls 50 feet high.

Over the years, the right to exercise was withdrawn or restored as a method of controlling this "difficult" prisoner who was liable to fits of rage and despair.

Obsession with Numbers

Because they are literally "doing time", counting the days, an obsession with numbers is something to which prisoners easily fall prey. Sade developed a mania for number codes and found "signals" in the correspondence he received from which he made weird calculations to predict the possible date of his release.

Had I not kept my son-in-law in prison, Lady Montreuil will say, could I have matched 5 s, 3 s and 8 s together, could I have fitted together 23 s and 9 s? And so arranged things that when my daughter first visits her husband, when she visits him for the last time and when she goes to fetch him, more than forty-eight numbers are the same?

Sade's mania for numbers had another source – a need to keep a tally of what he called **prestiges**, orgasms achieved through masturbation or the use of instruments provided by Renée.

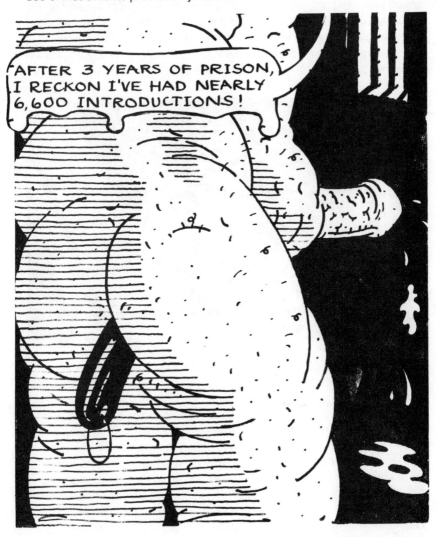

AFTER 3 YEARS OF PRISON, I RECKON I'VE HAD NEARLY 6,600 INTRODUCTIONS!

Sade also became pathologically jealous and accused the ever-faithful Renée of sexual infidelities with, among others, his former secretary Lefèvre. The dimensions of Lefèvre's penis are calculated from the date (5 August) of a letter Renée had sent him. "And there's the figure that fine fellow is classed with a 5, with a 7! which one supposes are his measurements."

A Dream of Laura

In a letter of February 1779 to Renée, Sade describes an extraordinary dream vision of his ancestress Laura de Noves. He had been reading the Abbé de Sade's life of Petrarch and the sonnets inspired by Laura. "My sole consolation here is Petrarch," Sade writes, and he continues, " . . . Laura turns my head; I am like a child, I read about her all day and dream about her all night. Listen to what I dreamt of her last night . . ."

"It was about midnight. I had just fallen asleep with those biographical jottings at my side. Suddenly she appeared to me . . . I could see her! The horror of the grave had not changed the brilliance of her charms, and her eyes still had the same fire as when Petrarch sang of them. She was completely draped in black muslin, her lovely fair hair flowing over it. As if to make her still beautiful, love tried to soften the essentially gruesome form in which she appeared to me. 'Why do you groan on earth?' she asked me. 'Come and join me. No more ills, no more worries, no more trouble in the vast expanse in which I live. Have courage and follow me there.' When she said this, I flung myself at her feet and addressed her, calling her 'my mother', and sobs shook me. She held out her hand to me and I covered it with my tears. Then she too wept. 'When I dwelt in that world which you loathe, I used to like to look into the future, multiplying my descendants till I reached you, but I did not see you so unhappy.' Then I was completely engulfed in my despair and affection, and flung my arms round her neck, to keep her with me, or to follow her and to water her with my tears. But the phantom vanished. All that remained was my grief."

The Formation of an Avant-garde Writer

This letter gives us an insight into Sade's literary transformation. Prison led him to channel his enormous energies into writing. Despite all the torments of his confinement, he was fortunate in being allowed to amass a large library and to study the most advanced scientific ideas of his time.

I READ THE ENCYCLOPÉDIE – 17 VOLUMES OF TEXTS AND 11 OF PLATES WHICH APPEARED BETWEEN 1751 AND 1772.

I EDITED THE WORK WITH D'ALEMBERT, A BRILLIANT MATHEMATICIAN AND ASTRONOMER, AND A CRITIC OF RELIGION AND THE CLERGY.

Denis Diderot (1713–84) essayist and thinker

DIDEROT AND I WERE BOTH MATERIALISTS.

Jean Le Rond d'Alembert (1717–83)

The Encyclopédistes and the Enlightenment

Other great contributors to the **Encyclopédie** included the philosophers Voltaire (1694–1778), whose satires savaged conventional morality, and Jean-Jacques Rousseau (1712–78), who argued that perfect human nature is corrupted by society. These and other **Enlightenment** thinkers were the intellectual forerunners of the French Revolution.

The attempt by the Encyclopédistes to provide a rational explanation of the universe drew down on it the hostility of the clergy (especially the Jesuits) and the official classes, its publication being twice prohibited. It was precisely its sceptical anti-religious tone that appealed to Sade.

But he didn't share the optimistic view of Diderot and Rousseau that human beings are naturally inclined to virtue, an innocence which is perverted by society. His own view was darker and more pessimistic.

Sade's interest in contemporary science extended to works by the naturalist Buffon (1707–88), whose **Natural History** describing the geological periods of the earth had been condemned by theologians, and Holbach (1723–89), the materialist and atheist philosopher, and by La Mettrie (1709–51), author of **L'Histoire Naturelle de l'Âme** (*Natural History of the Soul*).

For La Mettrie, man belongs to the animal kingdom with a "soul" that develops and decays with the body. As a materialist hedonist, he maintained that the pursuit of happiness is the main object of all activity and that there is no point in feelings of remorse.

LA METTRIE IS RIGHT. NATURE, NOT GOD, IS THE PRIME MOVER OF THE UNIVERSE.

NATURE IS IN A PERMANENT STATE OF MOTION — WHICH RECALLS THE FAMOUS SAYING OF THE 5TH CENTURY BC GREEK PHILOSOPHER HERACLITUS ...

EVERYTHING IS FLOWING.

Exploring the Human Animal

Sade was also interested in anthropology – the comparative study of human societies. This was an age of global exploration and he read the **Voyages** of Captain James Cook (1728–79) and those of the French explorer Bougainville (1729–1811), both of whom described the morals and customs of the Polynesian islanders.

Discipline and Punish

In 1782, after four years in Vincennes, Monsieur No. 6 was deprived of all books. The official reason stated was that books "overheated his head" and caused him to write "unseemly things". It was a severe blow. These "unseemly things" must have been found in the periodic searches of his cell.

Sade had by now taken a decisive step which broke with the conventions of his class. To be a dilettante writer of trifles was one thing, but to dedicate oneself to a *career* of writing was socially unacceptable for an aristocrat. Sade invested himself in his writing with all the passion and obstinacy that sustained him as a prisoner. Later, addressing himself to aspiring authors, he wrote . . .

"No one obliges you to exercise this as your profession; but if you undertake it, do it well. Above all do not choose it merely as a crutch to your existence; you work will reflect your needs, you will transmit your weakness into it; it will have the pallor of hunger: other professions will offer themselves to you: Make shoes but refrain from writing books."

One book denied him was Rousseau's autobiographical **Confessions** in which the author claimed to present a man "in all the truth of nature" down to his sexual abnormalities.

To forbid me this book is proof of truly discerning taste in my jailers. They do me the great honour to think that a Deist* author could possibly be a wicked book for me. I wish I were still at that stage!

*Deism acknowledges the existence of a non-personal God but rejects Scriptural revealed religion. God is seen as a beginning, like a watchmaker who makes and "winds up" the universe, then leaves it alone.

Dialogue between a Priest and a Dying Man

Sade demonstrated just how far in advance he was of the Encyclopédistes' Deism in his **Dialogue between a Priest and a Dying Man**, completed in 1782. Sade mainly differs from the Deists in his rigorous atheism. Diderot and d'Alembert, under attack from the Jesuits, had to be careful to cover themselves against the very serious charge of atheism. In their introduction to the 1751 edition, they felt obliged to disapprove strongly of atheism.

EVEN THE MOST TOLERANT OF MEN WILL NOT DENY THAT THE JUDGE HAS THE RIGHT TO REPRESS THOSE WHO PROFESS ATHEISM AND EVEN TO CONDEMN THEM TO DEATH IF THERE IS NO OTHER WAY OF FREEING SOCIETY FROM THEM.

Monsieur No. 6 felt he had nothing to lose in being more courageous. He challenged the need for a belief in God by putting into the dying man's mouth those arguments which clergymen have always found hard to answer.

This is a classic statement of scepticism and of the rule that a simple explanation consonant with all the known facts is to be preferred to a more elaborate one.

This introduces a constantly recurring theme in Sade's thought. Man has been formed by Nature in conformity with her own ends and needs, and she has an equal need for what we call "virtues" and "vices". It is in the workings of Nature that we find the unique cause of our "fickle human behaviour".

To be persuaded of the truth of a miracle, the dying man argues, he would have to be completely sure that the event was absolutely contrary to the laws of Nature, for only what is outside Nature can be considered a miracle. And who, he asks, "is so deeply learned in Nature that he can affirm the precise point where her domain ends and the precise point where its rules are broken."

Jesus, in his view, is no better than Muhammad, Muhammad no better than Moses and the three of them combined no better than Confucius "who did after all have some wise things to say". Religions are only good for setting man against man "and the mere name of these horrors has caused greater loss of life on earth than all other wars and all other plagues combined".

One of Sade's fundamental tenets is that our sexual dispositions are innate in us, placed there by Nature, therefore natural, therefore neither to be suppressed nor condemned.

Sade reveals himself a Manichaean. The 3rd-century Persian prophet Mani, or Manichaeus, taught that equal status and respect should be given to the positive and negative powers in the universe, that is, both to God and Satan – a belief which influenced many Christian heretical sects. Hinduism similarly worships the great goddess Kali who represents universal destructive power and whose devotees, the Thugs, at one time paid tribute to her by acts of ritual murder. And murder was one of Sade's obsessions.

THERE IS NOT A SINGLE VIRTUE WHICH IS NOT NECESSARY TO NATURE AND CONVERSELY NOT A SINGLE CRIME WHICH SHE DOES NOT NEED AND IT IS IN THE PERFECT BALANCE SHE MAINTAINS BETWEEN THE ONE AND THE OTHER THAT HER IMMENSE SCIENCE CONSISTS. BUT CAN WE BE GUILTY FOR ADDING OUR WEIGHT TO THIS SIDE OR THAT WHEN IT IS SHE WHO TOSSES US ON TO THE SCALES?

This too is an argument to which Sade will return again and again. Pushed to its limits, it poses the question whether there is any "crime" from sexual behaviour up to and including murder which can be condemned.

Sade, the thorough-going materialist, sees the example of Nature's perpetual generation and regeneration. Nothing perishes in this world, nothing is lost; man today, worm tomorrow; the day after tomorrow a fly; is this is not, he asks, to say that we keep on steadily existing? As for the belief that in an afterlife we shall have to give an account of our lives on earth and be judged on our record, he can see no basis for the idea of rewards and punishments.

The dialogue ends with the dying man – a hedonist to the last – explaining that he has six beautiful women waiting with whom he intends to share his last hours.

And so, the priest becomes one "whom Nature has corrupted because he had not succeeded in explaining what corrupt Nature is."

The Passionate Philosopher

Sade later denied authorship of the **Dialogue**, not surprisingly, for it was a dangerous document. But, in a letter to Renée, he made it clear that, although he might think it advisable to make a tactical denial, his convictions were unshaken. "My way of thinking is the fruit of my reflections; it derives from my existence, my way of organizing things. I am in no position to alter it; and, even if I were, I would not. This way of thinking . . . is my life's one consolation; it alleviates the sufferings of prison, it constitutes my pleasure in the world, and I am more attached to it than to my life."

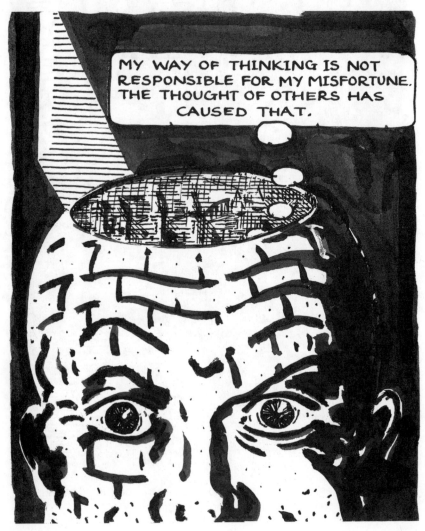

The Playwright

Before writing the **Dialogue**, Monsieur No. 6 busied himself with plays. He wrote seventeen while in prison which had titles like **The Two Twins or the Difficult Choice**, a two-act comedy in verse, **The Misanthrope through Love**, a five-act comedy in free verse, **Jeanne l'Aisné or The Siege of Beauvais**, a five-act tragedy in verse.

These texts were less daring than the **Dialogue** and he expressed himself optimistic about them to Renée.

The Novelist

Sade had also begun writing novels. For him, a novel was "any work of imagination fashioned from the most uncommon adventures which men experience in the course of their lives." He deeply admired the "vigorous" English novels, **The History of Tom Jones** by Henry Fielding (1707–54) and **Clarissa, or The History of a Young Lady** by Samuel Richardson (1689–1761), praising them for having "taught us that the profound study of man's heart – Nature's veritable labyrinth – alone can inspire the novelist whose work must make us see man . . . as he is capable of being when subjected to the modifying influences of vice and the full impact of passion."

MY NOVEL THE MISFORTUNE OF VIRTUE, LATER RETITLED JUSTINE, IS MODELLED ON BUT PARODIES RICHARDSON'S PAMELA.

Sade might also have known the pornographic novel **Fanny Hill** by John Cleland (1709–89), which appeared in 1750. His library contained Voltaire's **Candide** and **Zadig**, picaresque satires of society, and **Les Liaisons dangereuses** by Pierre Choderlos de Laclos (1741–1803), a detailed analysis of the libertine art of seduction.

"Vice and Passion" were certainly Sade's meat as a novelist, and what he called "Nature, even stranger than the moralists portray it to us," he said, "continually eludes the restricting limitations which their policy would like to impose."

Sade was fascinated by volcanoes to which he compares Nature from whose "constantly troubled bosom there rumble forth either precious stones serving men's needs or thunderbolts which annihilate them." His writing, he suggests, has the same elemental quality not easily suppressed.

The Liberty Tower of the Bastille

In 1784, the Vincennes fortress was closed and Sade was transferred to the infamous Paris Bastille. A hated symbol of royal tyranny, the Bastille in fact housed remarkably few, chiefly upper-class, prisoners who included a cardinal in Sade's time. He complained to Renée that conditions were worse than at Vincennes and continued to be a "bad" prisoner in conflict with his jailers over his right to exercise.

With time, however, and the help of his wife, he was able to assemble in his cell a library of six hundred books together with his numerous manuscripts and his own furniture.

64

In his five years there, Sade wrote at a furious speed. When in 1788 he drew up a catalogue of his work, it ran to fifteen octavo volumes – not including work hidden from his warders, in particular his Gothic chiller **The 120 Days of Sodom**, a masterpiece of what Sade defined as "a dissolute imagination such as has never been seen." Since it was liable to be confiscated on one of the routine searches of his cell, he made a fair copy of his draft on pieces of thin paper between 10 and 12 centimetres wide which he pasted together to form a roll over 12 metres long.

It took him thirty-seven days to make this final draft written in a microscopic hand on both sides of this roll.

THE FIRST NOVEL ON A ROLL OF TOILET PAPER?

The French Revolution

When in 1789 the revolutionary turmoil in Paris reached the streets round the Bastille, security was increased and exercise forbidden to the prisoners. In fury Sade shouted to the crowds outside through a megaphone improvised from a tin waste-pipe used for draining water and urine from his cell into the moat below.

This was the last straw for the Bastille commandant de Launay.

At dead of night, Sade was seized ("naked as a worm, with a pistol to my throat") and transferred to the Charenton lunatic asylum used by aristocratic families to confine – along with genuine cases of madness – persons whose behaviour was a social embarrassment. He was allowed to take nothing with him, neither his books nor his manuscripts.

When on 14 July 1789 the crowd stormed the Bastille, they killed the commandant, cut off his head and paraded it through the streets. They also sacked the place. Sade's belongings were looted. His wife, to his great annoyance, had delayed removing them. On hearing the news and being convinced that his work, in particular **The 120 Days**, had been destroyed, he "wept tears of blood".

One can replace beds, tables and commodes, but ideas never. The loss is beyond repair.

But the paper roll had survived somehow and was later found in his cell. It was published at last in 1904 by a Berlin psychiatrist Iwan Bloch under the pseudonym Eugène Dühren.

The 120 Days is a novel of the Gothic genre which originated in England in Sade's lifetime and was very fashionable and influential in France and Germany. This genre later gave us **Frankenstein** (1818), **Dracula** (1897) and Edgar Alan Poe's macabre stories written in the 1840s, many of which were later published together as **Tales of Mystery and Imagination**. Its modern descendant is the horror film. In the 1920s, the Gothic novel and Sade's work in particular were much admired by the Surrealist movement. Tristan Tzara, a founder of Dadaism, praised such fiction for its "love of ghosts, witchcraft, occultism, magic, vice, dreams, madness, passions, true or invented folklore, mythology (even mystification), social and other utopias, real or imaginary voyages, marvels, adventures, customs of savage peoples and generally everything that exceeded the rigid frame in which beauty had become fixed."

One Hundred and Twenty Days in the Château of Silling

Like any Gothic chiller, its location is typically romantic and timeless: the Château of Silling in the Black Forest, cut off from the world by impassable mountains. Sade describes how "it is impossible without great skill to go back down the mountain. Crossing a bridge you find yourself in a little plain surrounded on all sides by sheer crags rising to the clouds, crags which envelope the plain with a faultless screen. In the centre of this little plain is the Château of Silling." It is a location that cries out to be filmed.

The whole paraphernalia of portcullises, dungeons and torture

chambers, which are the normal trappings of the Gothic novel, may well derive from childhood memories of his uncle's château and from Sade's imprisonment in the Alps of Savoy or the fortress of Vincennes.

Nouveau Riche Characters

Sade sets his novel in the Thirty Years' War (1618–48), because at that time France saw "the emergence of the greatest number of those mysterious fortunes whose origins are as obscure as the lust and debauchery that accompanied them". Sade, the true "blue-blooded" aristocrat, chooses four members of this *nouveau riche* class for his leading characters, newly ennobled war profiteers, "bloodsuckers who are always on the watch for public calamities".

Sade excels at portraits of these ruthless men, for instance, the wealthy fifty-three-year-old banker Durcet, owner of Silling castle.

"He is small, short, broad, thickset, an agreeable, heavy face; a very white skin; his entire body and principally his hips and buttocks absolutely like a woman's; his arse is cool and fresh, chubby, firm and dimpled; his prick is extraordinarily small."

Durcet is joined by three partners in crime, known as "the friends"; a duke and his brother, who is a bishop, and a judge. Here is a description of the judge:

"a pillar of society; almost sixty years of age and worn by debauchery to a singular degree . . . he was tall, he was dry, had two blue lustreless eyes, a livid and unwholesome mouth, a long nose. Hairy as a satyr, flat-backed, with slack drooping buttocks that rather resembled a pair of dirty rags flapping upon his upper thighs; the skin of his arse was, thanks to whip strokes, so deadened and toughened that you could seize up a handful and knead it without his feeling a thing."

THE DUKE

THE JUDGE

THE BISHOP

The Friends' Conspiracy

These four libertines have brought with them three wives and the bishop's daughter who are all related in complicated and incestuous ways.

Sade's descriptions of beautiful women tend to be stereotyped ("lovely as a picture"), apart from that of Durcet's wife, who is the judge's daughter. She is described as having

"exceptionally large blue eyes, her nose thin and a little pinched at the top, her neck which is a shade long and attached in a singular way so that, through what appeared to be a natural habit, her head was ever so faintly bent towards her right shoulder especially when she was listening."

The Storytellers and Duennas

The libertine friends have also recruited four storytellers – middle-aged women, sexually experienced and criminal – and four duennas, older, downright ugly women with dark pasts whose task is to oversee two harems of eight girls and eight boys kidnapped by pimps from their parents. Desgranges, the fourth storyteller, is described as

"tall, thin, fifty-six, ghostly pale and emaciated, dead dull eyes, dead lips, she offered an image of crime about to perish for lack of strength. She had once upon a time been a brunette; there were some who even maintained she'd had a beautiful body, but it had become a mere skeleton capable of inspiring nothing but disgust. The skin on her hips was withered, marked, torn, more resembling marble paper than human skin."

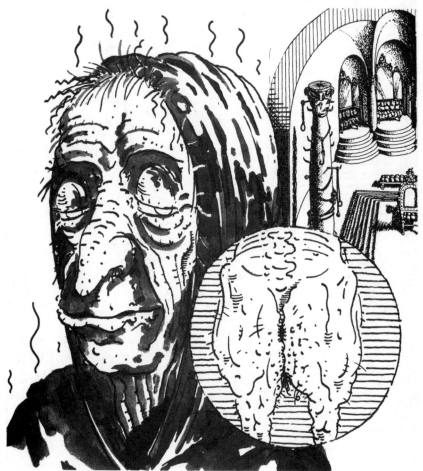

One of the duennas, Marie, fifty-eight years old,

"had almost no hair left, her nose stood askew, her eyes were dull and rheumy, her mouth large and filled with her thirty-two teeth, yes, they were all there, but all were as yellow as sulphur; she was tall, raw-boned, having whelped fourteen children, all fourteen of whom, said she, she had strangled out of fear that they would turn out ne'er-do-wells. Her belly rippled like the waves of the sea and one of her buttocks was devoured by an abscess."

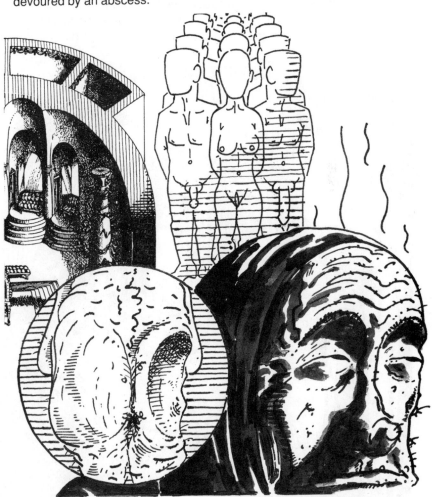

By contrast, the harems of sixteen young victims are said to be "beautiful" in an abstract way, mere fantasy objects of the libertines' lust. There are also eight sodomistic "fuckers", studs remarkable for the size of their penises.

Obsession with Arithmetic

The arithmetical symmetry that governs the composition of the seraglio and its attendants recalls Sade's obsession with numbers. It is reflected again in his description of the assembly room in the Château: "In shape it was semicircular; set into the curving wall were four niches whose surfaces were faced with large mirrors . . . these four recesses were so constructed that each faced the centre of the circle; the diameter was formed by a throne raised four feet above the floor and with its back to the flat wall, and it was intended for the storyteller; in this position she was well placed in front of the four niches intended for her auditors."

Timetables

The inmates of Silling are subject to Statutes, "articles of government" drawn up by the friends, which rigorously prescribe every detail of behaviour, dress, colours worn and varieties of sexual service expected of them.

Excremental Discipline

Excremental functions play an important part in the daily routines of Silling. Coprophilia and coprophagy are the libertines' common practices.

This kind of disciplinary control of the anal functions was in our own day imposed in a well-known English prep school, although admittedly the penalties were less severe.

WATER CLOSETS IN THE GIRLS' QUARTERS ARE TO BE SCRUPULOUSLY EXAMINED AFTER BREAKFAST.

IT IS FORBIDDEN TO RELIEVE YOURSELVES ELSEWHERE!

DELINQUENTS WHO CONTRAVENE THIS RULE ARE CONDEMNED TO DEATH!

What Is the Role of Storytelling?

In the context of their own life experiences, the storytellers give an exact account of "the passions". By these, Sade means "the extravagances of debauchery", beginning with the 150 "simple" perversions, continuing through the 150 complex ones to the 150 criminal and the 150 murderous ones. Each of these four autobiographies is to last thirty days, from 1 November to 28 February.

WE SHALL PROGRESS FROM AUTOEROTIC ASPHYXIATION...

... THROUGH NECROPHILIA AND PAEDOPHILIA...

... TO CLIMAX IN FEBRUARY...

...WITH STORIES OF MUTILATIONS BESTIALITY, CANNIBALISM AND KILLINGS.

These narrations are remarkable for occurring outside time, in unidentified spaces. The more terrible they are, the more impersonal they become, like notes to a treatise on human cruelty.

The Arithmetic of Death

What happens after the final storytelling – in a crescendo of orgies – is a sequence of horrendous tortures and murders inflicted on their victims by the four friends. By the end of the month, one subject is being dispatched daily. The arithmetic of death is spelt out in a Final Assessment of the inhabitants of the Château of Silling "in that memorable winter".

One is reminded of the bureaucratic returns of the SS murder squads at work in the ghettos of Eastern Europe. It is a tribute to Sade's power of imagination that he understood that human beings could be capable of such bookkeeping.

Massacred prior to the 1st of March in the course of the orgies	10
Massacred after the 1st of March	20
Survived and came back	16
Total	46

The obsession with numbers, the rigid schedules, the regimented tableaux of orgies are designed to control what is finally chaos, a mechanized frenzy of murder, in essence comparable to the complex killing machine of the Nazi extermination camps.

"All Hope Abandon, Ye Who Enter Here!"

Sade was perfectly aware of the extraordinary nature of his work. In the introduction he warns his "friend-reader", who is in a sense his accomplice (*mon semblable, mon frère*), that "you must prepare your heart and your mind for the most impure tale that has ever been told since our world began, a book the likes of which are met with neither amongst the ancients nor amongst us moderns . . . He who should succeed in isolating and categorizing these follies would perhaps perform one of the most splendid labours which might be undertaken in the study of manners, and perhaps one of the most interesting."

Can **The 120 Days** be judged merely a work of "imagination"? Sade's extreme depictions were excused by his first publisher, the German psychiatrist Iwan Bloch, on the grounds of "scientific importance to doctors, jurists and anthropologists" – a work to set alongside Kraft-Ebbing's famous and pioneering study of sexual pathology.

There is a more uncomfortable aspect to the work, found in the speech of the Duke de Blangis which introduces the unfortunate young girls to Silling, "feeble, enfettered creatures destined only for our pleasure". He reminds them that they are shut up in an impregnable citadel at the mercy of "beings of a profound and recognized criminality, who have no god but their lubricity, no laws but their depravity . . . godless, unprincipled, unbelieving profligates in whose eyes the life of a woman – the lives of all women – are as insignificant as the crushing of a fly."

Released?

Sade emerged from Charenton on Good Friday, 2 April 1790. The new Constituent Assembly decreed that all prisoners held under *lettres de cachet* should be liberated unless under sentence of death or insane.

So much in this period of social upheaval had radically changed. It was difficult being a *déclassé* aristocrat, an object of suspicion, a man without roots in the whirlwind of revolution. Changing with the times, abandoning the title which would have aroused suspicion, he now took on a new role and became "M. Sade, man of letters".

In this strange new world, he found himself free but penniless. He was also physically in a bad state, enormously corpulent for lack of exercise, having trouble with his eyes, plagued with migraines, rheumatism, gastritis and piles.

RENÉE WHO HAD SUSTAINED ME LOYALLY FOR SO MANY YEARS NOW REFUSED TO SEE ME !

Sade's wife, "after mature and carefully weighed consideration", applied for a separation and for the restitution of her large portion of the marriage settlement. She had been able to cope with separation but was apparently unable to face reunion. Her fear is understandable. A prisoner released after a long period in captivity is no longer the same person as went in.

Troubles at the Theatre

Sade turned to his first love, the theatre, to earn his living.

22 October 1791: first performance of a three-act play, **Count Oxtiern or the Effects of a Rake's Life**, an account of a kidnapping and rape by a Swedish nobleman, at the Théâtre Molière.

A newspaper critic praised it for its "vigour, but the character of Oxtiern is a revolting atrocity."

INTERRUPTIONS ON THE FIRST NIGHT ... PANDEMONIUM ON THE SECOND!

5 March 1792: Sade's play **Le Suborneur** (The Seducer) at the Théâtre Italien was noisily interrupted by Jacobin protesters wearing red Phrygian bonnets who had vowed to attack plays by ex-aristocrats.

Justine

In 1791, Sade published a revised and much enlarged version of the **Misfortunes of Virtue**, written in a few weeks in the Bastille, and renamed **Justine**. Like Richardson's **Pamela** and Cleland's **Fanny Hill**, it tells of the perils which confront a virtuous and innocent young girl.

Apology for Justine

Justine is dedicated to Marie-Constance Quesnet, a thirty-three-year-old actress whose husband had disappeared to America, leaving her with a young son. She and Sade entered into an affectionate relationship that lasted until his death twenty-four years later. He called her *la Sensible*, "the Sensitive One", with "the most judicious and enlightened of minds". To her, he explained the scheme of the novel, "the victory of Virtue over Vice".

IT IS NEW BECAUSE I PRESENT VICE TRIUMPHANT AND VIRTUE A VICTIM OF ITS SACRIFICES, EXPOSED TO EVERY FORM OF HUMILIATION AND CRUELTY WITH ONLY A SENSITIVE SOUL TO COMBAT THESE DANGERS.

Sade was anxious to forestall criticism. The opening paragraphs of the novel are a defensive apology.

"Will it not be felt that Virtue however beautiful becomes the worst of all attitudes when it is found too feeble to contend with Vice and that, in an entirely corrupted age, the safest course is to follow along after the others?... if misery persecutes virtue and prosperity accompanies crime, those things being as one in Nature's view, is it not far better to join company with the wicked who flourish than to be counted among the virtuous who founder?"

Virtue Severely Tested

Justine is an infinitely trusting young woman who never seems to learn from experience, an innocent simpleton like Voltaire's Candide, a parallel which Sade intended in order to raise important philosophical questions about society and morals.

Condemned for a crime she did not commit, Justine escapes and falls prey to every sort of male and female scoundrel, outlaw and exploiter. **Justine** is the horror novel version of Bertolt Brecht's **The Threepenny Opera** with its cast of underworld grotesques.

LEFT AN ORPHAN AND SEPARATED FROM MY SISTER, I FELL INTO ONE DISASTER AFTER ANOTHER.

She passes from a brothel to a community of depraved monks whose monastery resembles Silling. Whippings are served out to its young women inmates for trivial offences.

TWENTY STROKES FOR UNTIDY HAIR...

THIRTY FOR BEING LAZY IN THE MORNING!

It is a terrible parody of the idiocies of certain educational institutions, of short sharp shock camps, of military prisons, of "homes" where young inmates are "restrained", put in solitary confinement, abused verbally and sometimes physically.

Throughout all her experiences of torture and rape, Justine somehow preserves a notional "virginity". Falsely accused of theft, arson and poisoning, she is on her way to her execution when she is rescued by a gentleman and his mistress, who turns out to be her long-lost sister, Juliette. They take her off to live with them on their estate.

I WAS NOT BORN FOR SUCH FELICITY

Justine is killed in a great storm by a thunderbolt which strikes her in the breast. In a later more surreal version, the thunderbolt symbolically enters her mouth and emerges through her vagina. She is a victim to the end.

As in **The 120 Days**, descriptions of sex are brutally mechanical, cold as a police report. An example is the scene of anal intercourse in the dungeon of Roland, a monstrous counterfeiter, "hairy as a bear . . . his prick so big, so incredibly huge, that Justine had never seen anything like it." He combines sodomy with strangulation by a black silk cord round her neck. Justine "felt herself flooded with jets of sperm from the horrifying man who was buggering her; she heard the cries he uttered as he spilled it." Roland assures her that she felt only pleasure. Justine virtuously denies this.

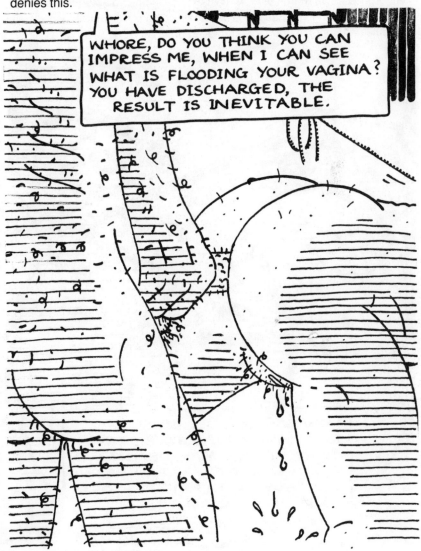

Concerning Justine's impregnable fantasy of virtue, Sade had this to say.

Justine's virtue makes of her an **object** with no relationship at all to the man (or woman) using her. Sade subverts conventional thinking by implying that sexual chauvinism (male or female) is the direct response to the virtuous object.

The height of ecstasy can be achieved only by the sight of that object undergoing "the strongest possible sensation" and "there is no more lively sensation than that of pain." What he calls "the voluptuous egoist" will therefore, when he has the power to do so, inflict "the strongest possible dose of pain upon the employed object."

HOW CAN A GIRL BE SO DULL-WITTED AS TO BELIEVE THAT VIRTUE MAY DEPEND ON THE SOMEWHAT GREATER OR LESSER DIAMETER OF ONE OF HER PARTS?

Sade is equally subversive about the moral order of society.

The callousness of the Rich legitimates the bad conduct of the Poor.

Robbery maintains a sort of equilibrium which totally confounds the inequality of property.

He who wishes to struggle alone against society's interests must expect to perish.

These are radical thoughts which remind one of the French anarchist Pierre Joseph Proudhon (1809–65) and his definition of property as theft. Less then admirable is Sade's assertion that foreshadows the Nazi logic of eugenic racial cleansing.

"The state can easily afford to be burdened by fewer people . . . bastards, orphans, malformed infants should be condemned to death immediately they are pupped."

Sade was far ahead of his time in defending sexual orientations that conflict with accepted prejudices. Persons with "curious tastes" are only acting in accordance with their organic structure and are no more guilty towards society than the blind or lame.

SOME DAY, WHEN THE STUDY OF ANATOMY IS PERFECTED, IT WILL BE POSSIBLE TO RELATE HUMAN BEHAVIOUR TO HUMAN TASTES.

Long before Freud, Sade understood fetishism. He compared it to the imagination which like a mirror reflects objects in many forms. An object may be unattractive, but, if it strikes the imagination in an agreeable manner, the object is loved, preferred, even if it has nothing really attractive about it.

Crime – or Nature in Motion

Sade is compulsively drawn to reflect on crime and especially murder. Murder has an almost aphrodisiac effect on his characters, because it is "the most infamous, the most forbidden of crimes that best arouses the intellect". But the intellect in this context is concerned with discovering how to achieve orgasm.

Sade begins from the concept of Nature as a force that cannot reproduce without committing acts of destruction. This is yet another example of his dialectical mode of thought – the same one that caused him to link life and death as two inseparable processes – and to see a contradiction at the heart of all existence. The argument then runs as follows.

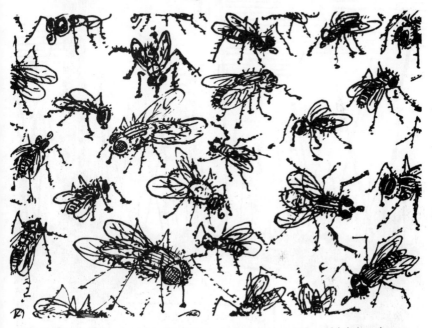

If Nature is involved in a constant process of renewal – which involves destruction – would we not be acting in harmony with her wishes if we were to keep on multiplying those acts of destruction? How can Nature possibly be angry when she sees man copying her and doing what she herself does every day? Following in the footsteps of La Mettrie, Sade believes that the primary and most beautiful of Nature's qualities is motion. Motion is constantly at work in Nature, but this motion is simply a perpetual sequence of crimes which destroy in order to regenerate. The result is a balance between destruction and regeneration. This equilibrium must be preserved; it can only be preserved by crimes; therefore crimes serve Nature.

Citizen Sade in 1792

Sade lived in one of the most radical areas of Paris known as Section des Piques, the "section armed with pikes", to which the revolutionary Jacobin leader Maximilien Robespierre (1758–94) belonged. Robespierre rose to supreme power and instigated the **Reign of Terror** (1793–94), infamous for its mass executions by the guillotine.

Sade was active in this "Pike Section", doing guard duty, organizing cavalry, reporting on the administration of the hospitals, proving himself a reliable citizen.

SO MUCH SO THAT I WAS APPOINTED MAGISTRATE!

As a magistrate, Sade deliberately helped several moderates to escape from the Terror. At this time, too, by a curious reversal of fortune, he was visited by his father-in-law who asked for his help at a difficult time.

Both of Sade's in-laws survived the Revolution.

"But justly . . . "

2 September 1792: When invasion by royalist émigré forces with foreign support threatened the Revolution, the rage of the Parisians led to the September massacres. In a letter to his Provençal lawyer Gaufridy, Sade deplores the "10,000 prisoners slaughtered on September 3rd. Nothing can equal the horror of the massacre committed (here Sade interpolated 'but justly' in case his letter was opened) . . . " Sade refers to the savage butchery of Princess de Lamballe.

ONE OF HER EXECUTIONERS CUT OFF HER *MONS VENERIS* AND STUCK IT ON HIS LIP AS A MOUSTACHE, MUCH TO THE HILARITY OF THE ONLOOKERS.

Sade was at this time serving in the 4th battalion, the 5th Legion of the National Guard, and appointed Secretary of the Section des Piques.

21 January 1793: "Louis Capet, aged 39, profession: last King of the French", was guillotined. Did Sade approve of the King's death? It is hard to know the precise nature of the politics of Sade, the survivalist "man of letters". In a letter to Gaufridy, 28 December 1791, Sade had this to say.

"I am an anti-Jacobin and hate them to the death; I worship the King, but I loathe the old abuses; I love very many articles of the constitution, but others revolt me; I want the nobility to be restored in its brilliance, for taking that away does no good; I want the King to be head of the nation; I do not want a national assembly, but two houses, as in England, which gives the King a modified authority balanced by the support of a nation necessarily divided into two orders – the third order [the clergy] *is useless, I want none of it. There you have my profession of faith. Now what am I? Aristocrat or democrat? Tell me, please, my dear lawyer, for I myself have no idea at all."*

Tribute to Marat

When the extremist Jacobin leader Jean-Paul Marat (1743–93) was murdered in his bath by Charlotte Corday from the right-wing Girondin party, Sade composed a tribute to his memory.

Sade delivered his speech at a public commemoration in the Place des Piques. His tribute was printed by the General Assembly of the Piques ward and distributed throughout France and to the armies. Was Sade being sincere?

THE MOST CHERISHED DUTY OF TRULY REPUBLICAN HEARTS IS THE RECOGNITION DUE TO GREAT MEN.

Abolition of Christianity.

15 November 1793: Sade headed a delegation to the National Convention to read a petition which proposed the abolition of Christian worship in churches and its replacement by the cult of Reason and Virtue.

"Tyranny and religious superstition were nurtured in the same cradle, both were daughters of fanaticism, both were served by those useless creatures known as the priest in the temple and the monarch on the throne: having a common foundation they could not but protect each other."

Unfortunately, Sade went too far in his atheism. A few days later, Robespierre, distancing himself from such radical thinking, announced that "atheism is aristocratic", and added that the idea of "a Great Being watching over us" was "essentially popular".

Under Arrest!

8 December 1793: Sade was taken to the Madelonnettes Prison. The warrant of arrest accused him of having applied in 1791 for service for himself and his sons in Louis XVI's Constitutional Guards – a charge punishable by the guillotine!

His situation was all the more dangerous because, at about the same time, through some confusion, his name had appeared on a list of émigrés. He had also shielded members of his own social class from prosecution.

YOU ARE ALSO CHARGED WITH BEING POLITICALLY MODERATE AND A MOST IMMORAL MAN, UNWORTHY OF SOCIETY.

MY RECORD OF SEXUAL TRANSGRESSIONS - AND WRITINGS - IS CATCHING UP WITH ME.

0000 0006

27 March 1794: After three prison transfers, Sade ends up in the Picpus hospital prison, in sight of the guillotine which had been moved from the Place de la Concorde because of complaints about the stink of blood. A drain for the blood now led to the Picpus charnel house. Sade described his experience of Picpus in a letter, "an earthly paradise, a lovely building, a magnificent garden, choice company, charming women, then all at once the guillotine is set up directly under our windows and they began to dispose of the dead in the middle of our garden . . . we buried 1,800 in thirty-five days".

Sade narrowly escaped the guillotine and was released the day after Robespierre was himself executed on 28 July 1794. What is the final verdict on Sade as "revolutionary citizen"? Did he adapt a mask of radicalism in order to survive?

It is difficult to believe that he could have sustained this charade so successfully for so long or produced political texts which convey more than merely conventional opinions.

An alternative explanation hinges on his position as a *déclassé* aristocrat who had suffered under the *ancien régime*, who knew the ruthlessness of the ruling class, to which he himself belonged, in dealing with those they considered deviants, who had himself experienced their "administration of justice". Persons who, as it were, drop out of their social class – as Sade now had – are like free molecules. They attach themselves to radical movements, whether of the Right or the Left. They bring with them immense contradictions in terms of their social attitudes. They are often highly intelligent but liable to kick over the traces, to be impatient of the accommodations required in the dangerous game of politics. They become ultra-radicals who refuse all compromise and call for a perpetual revolution. The political movements of the 1960s provided famous examples.

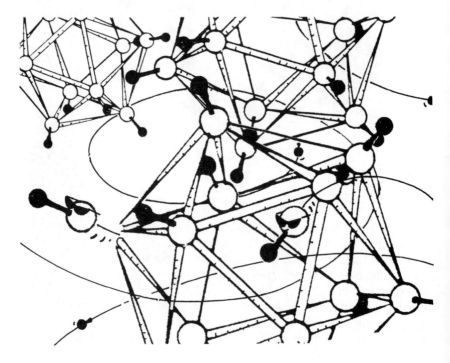

Under the five-man Directory which took power in 1795 after the Reign of Terror, Sade was free but marginalized, living in a state of considerable poverty. To raise money, he sold La Coste, which had been looted by the locals in a revolutionary outburst, but he never received the proceeds of the sale from his unreliable "man of affairs", the lawyer Gaufridy. With Mme Quesnet, he went from place to place, unsuccessfully trying to raise funds.

He ended up in a Versailles public hospital, dying of hunger and so cold "the ink froze in the inkwell".

Philosophy in the Bedroom

But even in those difficult times, he had not stopped writing daily. In 1795, his new publisher (the previous one had been guillotined) brought out a small two-volume work, with four erotic engravings, which the title-page claimed had been published in London. Although **Philosophy in the Bedroom** was written in the Revolution, its characters appear to belong to a society untouched by the events which happened during it. There is Madame de Saint-Ange, a widow of twenty-six and a libertine.

Her brother, Le Chevalier de Mirvel, twenty years old, like his sister a libertine and "amphibious".

Mme de Saint-Ange has a plot. It is to "educate" Eugenie de Mistival, a convent-bred virgin of fifteen, in the ways of unbridled libertine philosophy and sexual depravity. Eugenie is the daughter of a wealthy Parisian businessman whom Mme de Saint-Ange has seduced and who will therefore not object to this bedroom course in philosophy.

Brother and sister are joined by a third even more unscrupulous libertine named Dolmancé.

I PLAN THAT YOU, MY DEAR BROTHER, SHALL HARVEST THE MYRTLES OF CYTHEREA WHILE DOLMANCÉ PLUCKS THE ROSES OF SODOM. I SHALL HAVE TWO FORMS OF ENJOYMENT SIMULTANEOUSLY, THAT OF PERSONAL ENJOYMENT OF THESE CRIMINAL DELIGHTS AND THAT OF GIVING LESSONS IN THEM ...

"Dolmancé has just turned thirty-six; he is tall, extremely handsome, eyes very alive and very intelligent; but all the same there is some suspicion of hardness and a trace of wickedness in his features; he has the whitest teeth in the world, a shade of softness about his figure and in his attitude, doubtless owing to his habit of taking on effeminate airs so often; he is extremely elegant, has a pretty voice, many talents, and above all else an exceedingly philosophical bent to his mind."

FOR MY PLEASURES, I CARE ONLY FOR MEN, ALTHOUGH IN CERTAIN CIRCUMSTANCES AND ON MY OWN TERMS, I WILL HAVE INTERCOURSE WITH WOMEN.

The book is dedicated "To Libertines" because it appeals to their "passions" – Sade's word for sexual and other urges – which are merely "the means Nature employs to bring man to the ends she prescribes to him". But it is addressed also to women who are encouraged to take Mme de Saint-Ange as their model and to disregard anything that contradicts "pleasure's divine laws". The moral is that it is only by sacrificing everything to the pleasure of the senses that the individual, who never asked to be cast into this universe of woe, that this poor creature who goes under the name of Man, may be able to pick a few roses on the thorny path of life. It is a deeply pessimistic view of human destiny.

Mme de Saint-Ange sets out to demolish all of Eugénie's conventual notions of behaviour and morality: in short, to make the girl as criminal as she is herself.

The basic, practical demonstrations inspire Dolmancé to philosophical discourses on Man, Nature and God. "If matter acts, if Nature alone by reason of her energy is able to create, produce, preserve, maintain . . . what then becomes of the need to seek out a foreign agent?"

YOU MEAN THERE IS NO GOD?

NONE, AND AS FOR CHRISTIANITY, IT SHOULD HAVE BEEN UTTERLY DESTROYED BY RIDICULE AT THE START.

Eugénie is a willing pupil. She has discovered the joys of polymorphous sex and of daring speculation. But she still has reservations. Might some of the virtues prescribed by religion not perhaps contribute to our happiness? Dolmancé concentrates on charity and condemns the giving of alms and reveals himself a Thatcherite before his time.

THE INDIVIDUAL BORN IN MISFORTUNE OUGHT TO FEND FOR HIMSELF, SUMMONING UP ALL THE RESOURCES PUT IN HIM BY NATURE.

France, he explains, is threatened by overpopulation. That problem is merely aggravated if people help the poor. It is to free public schools and charitable establishments that they owe the terrible disorder in which they now live. (This is an extraordinary statement to make in the middle of the Revolution.)

Her body is hers and hers alone; she has the right to enjoy it as she sees fit. Adultery is justified by the tyrannical nature of marriage.

There are, however, certain problems connected with adultery. Eugénie's tutors propose practical solutions such as contraception, including the use of condoms, fellatio and anal intercourse.

It is a topic to which they return when Mme de Saint-Ange asserts that women should be the implacable enemies of "wearisome childbearing". If necessary, there is always abortion, which is an imaginary crime. Women are always mistresses of what they carry in the womb.

During a discussion of incest and of homosexuality, Dolmancé argues that both are natural, otherwise Nature would not have allowed us to find pleasure in them. Eugénie agrees that it is foolish to confuse laws and conventions which are social institutions with "Nature's divine ordinations".

BUT THAT RAISES THE PROBLEM OF MURDER...

NOTHING THAT DESTROYS CAN BE CRIMINAL, SUCH BEING THE LAW OF NATURE.

Dolmancé goes on to point out that while murder is forbidden to ordinary human beings, "an ambitious sovereign can at his ease and without the least scruple destroy the enemies prejudicial to his grandiose designs" and "cruel laws, arbitrary, imperious laws can every century assassinate millions of individuals".

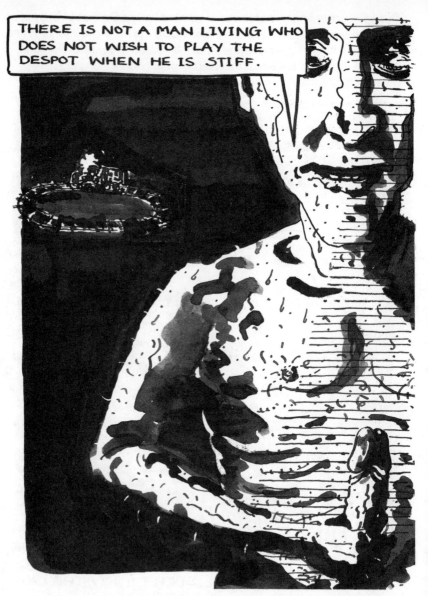

THERE IS NOT A MAN LIVING WHO DOES NOT WISH TO PLAY THE DESPOT WHEN HE IS STIFF.

Sade's most daring views are placed in the mouth of Dolmancé, such as those on the pleasures of inflicting pain. "What is it", he asks, "that one desires when taking one's pleasure? That everything around us be occupied with nothing but ourselves, think of nothing but us, care for us only. If the objects we employ know pleasure too, you can be sure they are less concerned for us than they are for themselves, and our own pleasure is consequently disturbed."

It is a frightening picture of male sexuality at the root of which, Dolmancé argues, lies cruelty. Men are more keenly affected by pain than by pleasure, whereas women are less susceptible to pain as a sexual stimulus. Calling on anthropology to buttress his argument, Dolmancé asserts that cruelty exists among savages who are much closer to Nature than civilized men. We are all born with "a dose of cruelty which education later modifies". But education goes against Nature.

CRUELTY IS SIMPLY THE ENERGY IN A MAN WHOM CIVILIZATION HAS NOT YET ALTOGETHER CORRUPTED. IT IS THEREFORE NOT A VICE BUT A VIRTUE.

There is a distinction to be made, however, between two forms of cruelty. The one comes from stupidity. It is by its nature unreasonable and turns the thinking being into a beast. The other variety of cruelty is "the fruit of extreme organic sensibility". People who are cruel in this way are extremely delicate.

IF THEY ARE DRIVEN TO EXTREMES OF CRUELTY, THEIR GOALS ARE DETERMINED BY INTELLIGENCE AND NICENESS OF FEELING - IN SHORT BY THEIR SENSITIVITY. CRUELTY LIBERATES THEIR FEELINGS.

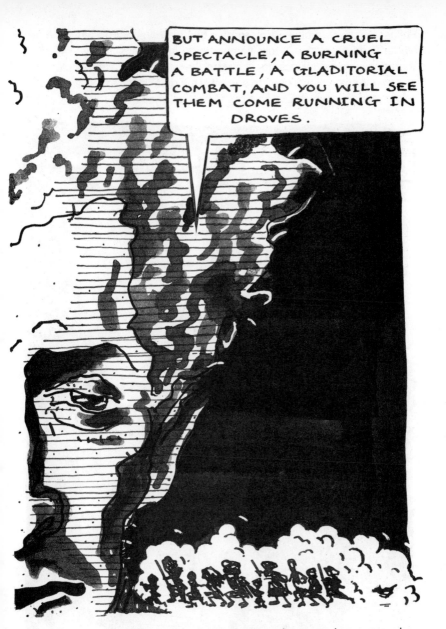

BUT ANNOUNCE A CRUEL SPECTACLE, A BURNING A BATTLE, A GLADITORIAL COMBAT, AND YOU WILL SEE THEM COME RUNNING IN DROVES.

It is this kind of cruelty that one finds, Dolmancé argues, in women who are unfortunately inhibited by society and can only surrender in very special circumstances to their inclinations because these run counter to society's idea of femininity.

These are rare occasions however; women must usually contain themselves and suffer.

Philosophical instruction is interrupted by the arrival of Eugénie's mother, Madame de Mistival, a lovely woman "thirty-two at most". The assembled libertines, which now includes the gardener's boy, Augustine, a stud with an enormous prick, proceed to submit Mme de Mistival to extremes of sexual abuse in which Eugénie enthusiastically joins.

In final humiliation, Mme de Mistival is raped front and rear by Dolmancé's valet Lapierre whose penis is eaten away by a syphilitic chancre. Eugénie then proceeds to sew up her mother's genitalia and anus.

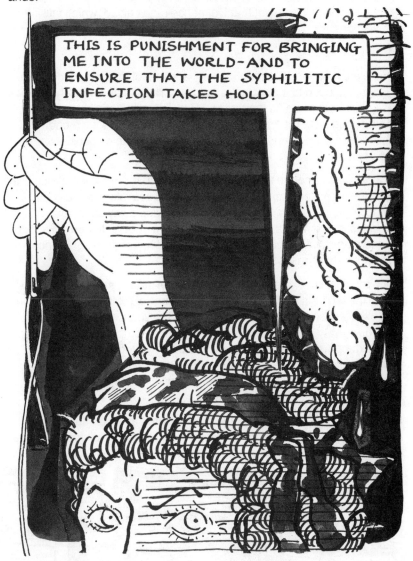

A terrible and savage conclusion to a fantasy which forces us to wonder – is it hatred of Sade's own mother, or indeed of his mother-in-law Mme de Montreuil, that is expressed here?

"French, one more effort, if you want to be Republicans!"

Embedded in these "boudoir" dialogues is a political address to the French people, a pamphlet that Dolmancé reads aloud, which falls into two sections.

1. Religion

People must understand that "in every age one of the primary concerns of kings has been to maintain the dominant religion as one of the political bases that best sustains the throne." Religion is by definition incompatible with a libertarian regime. Once good laws have been passed, however, a republican society will be able to dispense with religion.

"A people wise enough and brave enough to drag an impudent monarch from the heights of grandeur to the foot of the scaffold, that has been able to vanquish so many prejudices and sweep away so many ridiculous impediments will be wise and brave enough to abolish a mere phantom after having successfully beheaded a real king." Ignorance and fear are the twin bases of every religion.

Once the final blow against religion has been struck, state education will see to the rest, building on a sound ethical basis, replacing superstition with excellent social principles, instructing the young on their duties towards society. There is a utilitarian argument for the value of morals – good examples will make good citizens of the young and then "true patriotism will shine in every spirit". When this work has been accomplished in France, another generation will take over until it becomes a universal law.

Sade's fear that Christianity would be reinstated as a counter-revolutionary basis of tyranny within ten years proved well-founded when Napoleon was crowned Emperor in the cathedral of Notre Dame.

2. "Manners"

A new government requires new "manners" – that is, new ways of behaviour that will be relevant to a new society. In such a society, there must be freedom of conscience and freedom of the press. The corollary is that there must be freedom of action too. This will lead to a reduction in crime because there are "very few criminal actions in a society whose foundations are liberty and equality". In a free society, laws should be lenient and few in number. In that way, all men, whatever their character, will be able to observe them. The legal system should, however, take into account that some people may be unable to obey its laws – here he is clearly thinking of sexual behaviour – and should therefore be exempt. To force them to conform would be like trying to force the blind to distinguish one colour from another.

Laws should therefore be flexible and mild. Above all, he argues for the abolition of capital punishment which is "impractical, unjust, inadmissible". Passion – strong feelings – have no place in law. Such feelings can justify murder in an individual – people can be carried away by their feelings as in a *crime passionel*. But the law has – or should have – no feelings, no emotions, no such excuse, and cannot therefore be justified in taking a person's life. In any case, capital punishment has never repressed crime. "Crime is every day committed at the foot of the scaffold." The system of putting a man to death for killing another causes us to end up with not one but two men less. "Such arithmetic is in use only among headsmen [executioners] and fools."

How to Deal with Crimes

Crimes can be reduced to four headings: calumny, theft, crimes "caused by impurity", and murder which he intends to examine "with a philosopher's torch". Aware of embarking on a dangerous course, Dolmancé enters a caveat to excuse and justify his decision.

"Let no one tax me with being a dangerous innovator; let no one say that by my writings I seek to blunt the remorse in the evildoers' hearts, that my human ethics are wicked because they augment those evildoers' penchant for crime. I wish formally here and now to certify that I have none of these perverse intentions; I set forth the ideas which, since the age when I first began to reason, have identified themselves in me and to whose expression and realization the infamous despotism of tyrants has been opposed for uncounted centuries. So much the worse for those susceptible to corruption by ideas."

Calumny – libel and slander – is quickly dismissed.

Legislators would find it difficult to justify a law that punished it. They ought, on the contrary, to encourage and reward it.

TO BE SLANDERED IS A TEST OF PURITY FROM WHICH THE VIRTUOUS MAN EMERGES WITHOUT STAIN.

Theft

Theft, he asserts in familiar terms, distributes wealth more evenly and can therefore scarcely be branded a crime under a government that aims at equality.

What, he asks, are the elements of the social contract? And answers that it consists in yielding a little of one's freedom and wealth to assure and sustain the preservation of the other's. He is therefore critical of the pledge to respect property which the Nation has just required all citizens to subscribe to under oath. This must lead to barbarous inequality.

IT CANNOT BE A JUST LAW THAT ORDERS A MAN WHO HAS NOTHING TO RESPECT ANOTHER WHO HAS EVERYTHING.

Crimes of Impurity

The crimes of so-called "impurity" are prostitution, incest, rape and sodomy. These are all considered "moral" crimes, but in Dolmancé's view it is a very good thing that the individual citizen is not moral.

WHY IS THAT?

BECAUSE THE TENSION CREATED BETWEEN THE CITIZEN AND THE VALUES OF THE SOCIAL ESTABLISHMENT LEADS TO INSURRECTION.

Permanent Insurrection

Insurrection is indispensable to a political system of perfect happiness – that is to say a system which like the French republican government will be the subject of hatred and envy for all its foreign neighbours. Immoral man is in a state of perpetual unrest which encourages him to promote permanent insurrection – a state in which the true republican must always keep his government.

Dolmancé's "manifesto" looks ahead to the idea of "permanent revolution" advocated by Trotskyist movements of the 1960s and looks far back to the millenarian revolutionaries who prophesied that the bonds of law would be loosened, human instincts set free and human beings allowed to seek fulfilment of their deepest urges. Dolmancé (or Sade) emerges politically as an anarchist – one in a long chain of libertarian thinkers.

"Impurities" cannot be judged criminal and should be allowed expression instead of being persecuted. Establishments should be set up where fundamentally despotic fancies can be acted out legally and in comfort. The customers will leave satisfied and calmed. If their passions are blocked they will find other outlets and cause trouble to the republic.

I AM NATURALLY INTERESTED IN ESTABLISHING THE RIGHT TO FORMS OF SEXUAL BEHAVIOUR TO WHICH I AM MYSELF INCLINED AND WHICH ARE DUE TO THE PROMPTINGS OF NATURE.

Are these really Sade's own personal views, for which Dolmancé's pamphlet-reading acts only as the mouthpiece? Or are these rather Sadeanist provocation that take republicanism to its extreme logical conclusions? Interestingly, these Sadeanist ideas were not forgotten. During the Revolution of 1848, this appeal to the French people to make "another effort to be republicans" was reprinted and distributed – the same year as another immensely influential pamphlet, **The Communist Manifesto** of Karl Marx and Friedrich Engels.

Juliette or the Prosperities of Vice

In 1797, **La Nouvelle Justine**, a revised and much enlarged version of **Justine** (1791), was published anonymously. Sade's new title is an obvious mocking reference to Jean-Jacques Rousseau's **La Nouvelle Hélöise**, a widely popular, influential, romantic (not to say sentimental) attempt to assert the natural goodness of human beings. The descriptive title of this long picaresque odyssey of virtue and vice is **The New Justine or the Misfortunes of Virtue followed by the History of Juliette, her sister**.

A Portrait Gallery of Villains

Juliette tells her story which begins when she is a convent girl in Panthémont Nunnery. The abbess, Mme Delbène, has no religious vocation but was placed there at the age of twelve to save on her dowry that will further enrich her brother. Mme Delbène indulges in orgies with the girls which Juliette rapturously enjoys.

IN BETWEEN SUCH EPISODES, THE ABBESS INSTRUCTED ME IN LIBERTINE PHILOSOPHY.

THE UNIVERSE RUNS ITSELF AND THE ETERNAL LAWS IN NATURE SUFFICE WITHOUT ANY FIRST CAUSE OR PRIME MOVER TO PRODUCE EVERYTHING WE KNOW.

Mme Delbène's philosophy is the familiar Sadean one. For instance, conscience for the abbess is merely prejudice instilled by education, a code which is subject to historical changes, local laws and geography. As for God, there is none.

The abbess sees in the universe no start, no finish, no fixed boundaries; it is an incessant passing from one state to another. Both in philosophy and in her sex education, Juliette is a fast learner.

In the Brothel

Juliette's first harsh lesson is immediate expulsion from the convent on the bankruptcy and death of her parents.

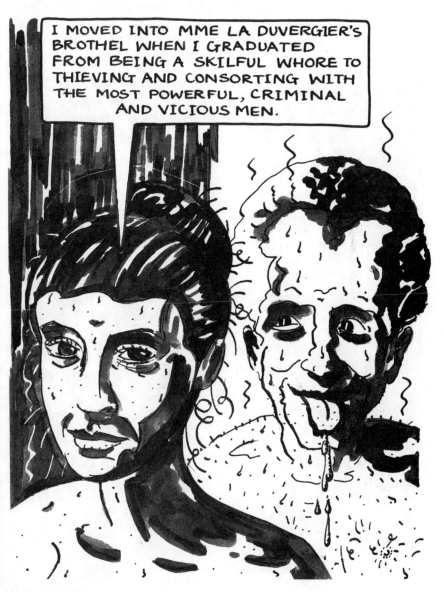

In this way, she meets a government minister, Monsieur de Saint-Fond, "most false, most treacherous, most depraved, most savage, of infinite hauteur, possessed of the art of robbing France to the highest degree."

Monsieur de Saint-Fond

Saint-Fond puts the criminally talented Juliette in charge of his orgies. Thirty victims a month perish in his lecherous dinner parties, girls being roasted like chickens on a spit. In a paroxysm of debauchery, Saint-Fond organizes the poisoning of his father, buggers his own daughter at the dying man's bedside, then hands her over to his loathsome associate Noirceuil. He then exults in this Sadean arithmetic of crime.

I HAVE COMMITTED PATRICIDE, I MURDERED, I PROSTITUTED, I SODOMIZED.

Mass Extermination

Saint-Fond believes France faces the grave problems of overpopulation and the spread of education, a combination which he fears might lead to revolution. His solution rivals in its appalling logic Jonathan Swift's **Modest Proposal** to resolve Ireland's poverty by rearing Irish babies as meat for export.

MY PLAN IS TO DEVASTATE FRANCE BY SIEZING ALL THE FOODSTUFFS AND FORCE TWO-THIRDS OF THE COUNTRY INTO STARVATION AND CANNIBALISM.

Even for Juliette, this is too much. Her shudder of pity infuriates Saint-Fond. Too late, she cries, "Ah, fatal virtue, I have once been deceived by you!" It will not happen again, but now she must escape from Saint-Fond.

Lady Clairwil's Society of Crime

Juliette marries the elderly Count de Lorsange for his money, has a daughter by him, then poisons him. She joins forces with the magnificent, exceptionally talented and fearsome Englishwoman, Lady Clairwil, who adores "avenging my sex for the horrors men subject us to" by murdering her oppressors. Lady Clairwil enrols Juliette in the "Sodality of the Friends of Crime". The Sodality is based on the firmly held, atheistic view that "man is not free and that, bound absolutely by the laws of Nature, all men are slaves of these fundamental laws."

The forty-five clauses of the Sodality's rule book is an extraordinary document to read. Not only does it reveal again Sade's mania for detailed order but is also a parody, a striking example of the black humour that occasionally relieves the horror of his stories.

Clairwil is one of a gallery of powerful, intelligent, active women with whom Juliette has important relationships: Durand, an astrologer and poisoner, who becomes Juliette's business partner, and the Princess Olympe de Borghese, an incendiarist and lesbian, whose orgies are attended by dwarfs, animals, hermaphrodites and other oddities are like scenes from a Fellini film.

Travels in Italy

On the run still from the vengeful Saint-Fond, Juliette travels extensively in Italy as a rapacious tourist, retracing Sade's own exile there "in the land of Nero". In the Apennines, she stays in the Silling-like castle of a Russian, Minski, a cannibalist giant.

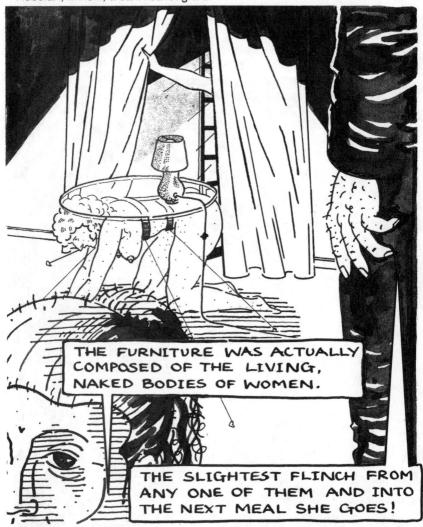

THE FURNITURE WAS ACTUALLY COMPOSED OF THE LIVING, NAKED BODIES OF WOMEN.

THE SLIGHTEST FLINCH FROM ANY ONE OF THEM AND INTO THE NEXT MEAL SHE GOES!

Sade has anticipated the sculpture of Allen Jones in the 1960s whose figures of half-naked women serve as chairs and tables. Minski has invented a machine which can stab and decapitate sixteen captives – all women, naturally – in one operation. Juliette skilfully escapes unharmed from this monster's den.

The Pope

The climax of her conquests in Italy is Pope Pius VI. "I was on fire", she says, "to see the Pope's prick." But before he can have sex with her, she requires from him "a philosophical dissertation on murder".

Murder, His Holiness explains, is in fact no crime, for murderers are as much part of Nature as are war, famine and plague.

YOU WILL ALWAYS FIND WRONGS MEASURED NOT BY THE SIZE OF THE OFFENCE BUT BY THE VULNERABILITY OF THE AGRESSOR; AND THERE IS YOUR EXPLANATION WHY WEALTH AND POSITION ARE ALWAYS RIGHT AND INDULGENCE IS ALWAYS AT FAULT.

In a splendid piece of Sadean irony, the Pope delivers a materialist discourse on the universe. In this lecture, different from and in contradiction to Sade's previously held views, the view that the Pope proclaims is that man has no relationship to Nature nor Nature to man. It is true that Nature as it evolved has produced man but once produced he is subject to his own laws which are those of self-preservation and reproduction.

The whole long discourse is remarkable for passages on human destiny, the fate of the planet, the absolute interdependence of the animal, mineral and vegetable kingdoms and the meaning of death.

IN ALL LIVING BEINGS, THE PRINCIPLE OF LIFE IS NOT OTHER THAN THAT OF DEATH.

This is a profoundly dialectical statement and looks forward to Sigmund Freud's concept of *thanatos* or the Death Instinct: "the aim of all life is death."

With the long philosophical foreplay over, the Pope has sex with Juliette behind the altar in St Peter's.

It is followed by an orgy in the Sistine Chapel, during which Juliette's accomplices contrive to steal a huge sum of money from the Pope's treasury. "I did not see His Holiness again," she comments. "He felt, I suspect, that my visits to the Vatican were a little more than he could afford."

Against Nature

There arises the question of why the blasphemous desecration of the communion wafer figures so often in Sade's life and fictions. What satisfaction does an atheist obtain from an action which cannot challenge his non-existent faith? Is he really deep down a believer, as the Church might hope and hence reclaim him? Sade's answer is this: "Three-quarters of Europe attaches very religious ideas to the host" and to read of its desecration causes the devout reader to suffer moral torture. Sade's views on good and evil in nature and in human beings – his Manichaeism – has been used to reclaim him for orthodox religion, but his rejection of Christianity was complete. For him, Nature alone had a moral validity. The problem was that Nature, sovereign Nature, was unchallengeable. The impossibility of outraging Nature was man's greatest torture.

I SHOULD LIKE TO UPSET HER PLANS, BLOCK HER ADVANCE, STOP THE STARS IN THEIR COURSES, THROW OFF THEIR BALANCE THE SPHERES WHICH FLOAT IN SPACE, DESTROY WHATEVER IS USEFUL TO HER, PROTECT WHATEVER IS HARMFUL TO HER, BUILD UP WHATEVER ANNOYS HER, IN A WORD INSULT HER IN ALL HER WORKS.

Sade's outburst of impatience against Nature is echoed by Lady Clairwil's unappeasable wish for the "perfect crime". "What I should like to find is a crime, the effects of which would be perpetual, even when I myself do not act, so that there would not be a single moment of my life, even when I was asleep, when I was not the cause of some chaos, a chaos of such proportions that it would provoke a general corruption or a disturbance and that even after my death its effects would still be felt."

Juliette's reply is Sade's own self-ironic admission of ambition and failure. A grandiose way of confirming that he was of no use except as a writer.

Verdicts on Juliette

The avant-garde modernist poet Guillaume Apollinaire (1880–1918) judged Sade prophetic.

"Justine is a woman as she has been up till now, enslaved, miserable and less than human, Juliette represents the woman whose advent he (de Sade) anticipated, a figure of whom minds have as yet no conception, who is rising out of mankind and who will renew the world."

Margaret Crosland, translator and an authority on Sade, speaks of Juliette as "a maitresse-femme, an early and repulsive representation of fantasy feminism". No woman can read Juliette without a shudder of confusion.

The novelist Angela Carter sees Juliette as a more positive representation of liberated woman.

COULD I ACHIEVE THE NECESSARY POWER OVER MYSELF AND OTHERS TO COMMIT CRIMES OF THIS ATROCIOUS MAGNITUDE?

WOMEN SHOULD NOT BE SEEN ONLY AS DAUGHTERS OR WIVES, SUBJECT TO MEN, AND EXPECTED TO USE THEIR SEX PRINCIPALLY FOR THE PROCREATION OF CHILDREN.

Nevertheless, Sade does not break free from the ideology of his time and the habits of a *grand seigneur* which took women to be subject to men.

Under Arrest, Again!

6 March 1801: That day, while Sade visited the offices of his publisher, Nicolas Massé, the police suddenly arrived, searched the premises and found various manuscripts and copies of **Juliette**.

Massé informed the police where the remaining stock of **Juliette** was kept and this was destroyed. Sade insisted he was only the "copyist" of the manuscript, not its author.

What was the reason for Sade's arrest? It has been wrongly alleged that Sade was the author of **Zoloé**, an obscene pamphlet pillorying Napoleon, his wife Josephine and others of the ruling group. The true reason remains mysterious, but the familiar result is that Sade was once again imprisoned without trial because the authorities decided that a "trial would cause too much scandal which an exemplary punishment would still not make worthwhile".

SO, I MUST AGAIN SUFFER "ADMINISTRATIVE PUNISHMENT" UNDER THE REGIME OF OUR FIRST CONSUL, NAPOLEON.

27 April 1803: Transferred from the Sainte Pélagie to Bicêtre prisons, Sade finally ended up back in Charenton insane asylum, thanks to persuasion from his family, where it was officially recommended that he be permanently locked up.

Theatre for the Insane

For its day, Charenton was a relatively enlightened asylum. Its director, Monsieur de Coulmier, a former priest and an intelligent humane man, befriended and protected Sade.

COULMIER PERMITS ME TO STAGE MY OWN PLAYS WITH INMATES AS MY ACTORS.

These performances attracted a fashionable audience, perhaps for reasons of voyeuristic curiosity, such as brought contemporary Londoners to visit the Bedlam asylum on Sunday afternoons.

Coulmier gave a positive and progressive reply to official criticisms of these theatrical events, "seeing in lighter drama a therapeutic method for the deranged."

HE ALSO ALLOWED MARIE-CONSTANCE QUESNET TO JOIN ME AT HER OWN REQUEST.

This was proof of Mme Quesnet's devotion to Sade, just as it is a sign of Sade's devious character that he passed her off as his daughter.

Persecuted to the End

Sade would remain confined in Charenton for eleven years, until his death. His family paid for his upkeep in the institution.

Throughout that period he continued to write, producing a ten-volume work called **The Days of Florabelle**, which was confiscated by the police during one of their routine searches of his room along with several other manuscripts. **Florabelle** the author would never see again. After his death, it was handed to his son who burned it.

ENDLESS ATTEMPTS WERE MADE TO TRANSFER ME BACK TO PRISON ON THE GROUNDS THAT MY ONLY MADNESS IS THAT OF VICE!

Napoleon's Decision

In 1810, the case of Sade was referred to Napoleon himself who found it important enough to bring before his Privy Council.

Napoleon personally signed the decision to keep Sade in detention and denied all communication with the outside world. Count de Montalivet, Minister of the Interior, also decreed that he was to be segregated from the other inmates and above all not to be allowed to use "pencils, pen, ink or paper". To deprive him of writing materials was an act of deliberate cruelty.

REPORTS ON SADE DESCRIBE HIM AS "IN A PERPETUAL STATE OF LASCIVIOUS FURORE, WHICH CONSTANTLY COMPELS HIM TO MONSTROUS THOUGHTS AND ACTIONS..."

Coulmier, writing as "head of a humanitarian institution", bravely defended Sade who, stubbornly unrepentant, went on writing to the end.

AH, MA CHÈRE PETITE MADELEINE I AM SUBJECTED TO CONSTANT INTERROGATIONS. WHAT FOR? TO ESTABLISH MY STATE OF MIND FOR A RETURN TO PRISON.

Sade became intimate *circa* 1808 with teenaged Madeleine Leclerc, a domestic employee at Charenton, whose visits and occasional sexual favours he recorded in his diaries almost up to his death.

7 July 1810: Sade's wife, Renée, blind and obese for some considerable time, died at the Château of Echauffour.

The writer Charles Nodier recorded a description of Sade in old age, unwell and enormously fat which "prevented him from displaying the last traces of grace and elegance, still discernible in his manners. Yet his tired eyes still preserved something of brilliance and finesse which glowed in them from time to time like a dying spark among extinct embers."

11 APRIL 1814 – ABDICATION OF NAPOLEON. 3 MAY 1814 – RETURN OF KING LOUIS XVIII TO PARIS...

From Sade's Last Testament

On 2 December 1814, before another decision to transfer him to prison could be made, Sade quite suddenly died.

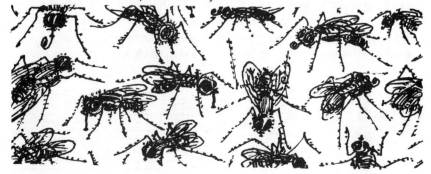

I forbid my body to be opened under any pretext whatsoever. I demand with the greatest insistence that it should be kept forty-eight hours in the room where I shall die, placed in a wooden coffin which will be nailed down only after the forty-eight hours referred to above, on the expiration of which the said coffin will be closed; during this time a dispatch shall be sent to the Sieur Le Normand, wood merchant, boulevard l'Égalité No. 101 at Versailles, asking him to come himself together with a wagon to take my body in order to transport it under his escort to the wood on my estate at Malmaison in the commune of Émancé near Épernon where I want it to be placed without any form of ceremony in the first overgrown thicket which is found on the right in the said wood as you come into it on the side of the old castle by the wide alley which divides the wood in two. My grave shall be dug in this thicket by the farmer of Malmaison under the inspection of Monsieur Le Normand, who shall not leave my body before it has been placed in the said grave. He can be accompanied during the ceremony, if he wishes, by those among my relatives or friends who without any show of mourning who will want to give me this last sign of attachment. Once the grave has been filled in it shall be sown over with acorns so that afterwards the ground of the said grave having been replanted and the thicket being overgrown as it was before, the traces of my tomb will disappear from the surface of the earth, as I flatter myself that my memory will be effaced from the minds of men, except none the less from those of the small number of people who have been pleased to love me up to the last moment and of whom I carry into the grave a most tender recollection.

Made at Charenton-Saint-Maurice when of sound mind and in good health, January 30th, 1806.

signed D. A. F. Sade

Sade's Legacy

"The Divine Marquis" has not lacked for advocates. An important one was Charles Baudelaire (1821–67), founder of French Symbolist poetry, whose only collection of poems, **Les Fleurs du Mal** (Flowers of Evil), led to his conviction for obscenity under the regime of Napoleon III, nephew of the first.

He shared Sade's view that sin was the natural state of human nature and sex was a Sadean business. "In the act of love, there is a great resemblance to torture or a surgical operation." Baudelaire linked *ennui* – overwhelming boredom – with the urge to do evil for evil's sake.

ONE MUST ALWAYS COME BACK TO SADE, THAT IS TO SAY TO NATURAL MAN, TO EXPLAIN EVIL.

Sade is the shadowy inspirational figure behind much 19th-century French Romanticism and Naturalism.

Victor Hugo (1802–85) and Alexandre Dumas (1802–70) have been called "relations of Sade who throw a morsel of his debauches into their productions".

ALEXANDRE DUMAS

GUSTAVE FLAUBERT

The paintings of Eugène Delacroix (1798–1863) with their taste for slaughter (especially of naked women) are in the Sadean tradition. Gustave Flaubert (1821–80) is described as "an intelligence haunted by Sade" whom he admired immensely.

Surrealism

Sade's legacy extends to Surrealism via a chain of audacious 19th-century authors – Count de Lautréamont, Arthur Rimbaud, Friedrich Nietzsche, Alfred Jarry and others – coupled with a turn-of-the-century psychiatric interest in sexual pathology and the rise of Freudian psychoanalysis. Surrealist art and writing represented a powerful stream of modernism that wished to reach into the unconscious and bring to the surface images that were unhesitatingly accepted no matter how strange or shocking. André Breton (1896–1966) wrote in the Second Surrealist Manifesto of 1930 . . .

SADE IS A SURREALIST IN HIS SADISM!

Paul Éluard (1895–1952), one of the finest of modern French poets and a leading figure in the Surrealist movement, saw in Sade a positive figure. "Sade", he wrote, "wished to give back to civilized man the force of his primitive instincts and to liberate the amorous imagination from its fixations. He believed that in this way and in this way only would true equality be born."

Luis Buñuel (1900–83), the Spanish Surrealist film-maker, used Sade's **The 120 Days of Sodom** to produce his film **L'Age d'Or** (1930) which was anticlerical and deeply critical of bourgeois values and politics. Buñuel shared Sade's insistence that our cruel imaginings ought not to be suppressed.

The final sequence of the film begins with a long shot of the Château of Silling from which – a caption tells us – the survivors of the criminal orgies are departing. As the great doors slowly open, the head of a bearded man, dressed "like a Hebrew of the first century", appears, clearly Jesus, who for Sade was an ineffectual prophet, preaching a ridiculous message of submission to power.

A slightly longer shot reveals the Duke who waits for his companions to join him. A young girl of about thirteen appears clutching her breast with a blood-stained hand. She falls exhausted on the threshold. The Duke picks her up and helps her back into the castle. After a pause, there is a terrible shriek from inside, then the Duke re-emerges and is followed by his three fellow-orgiasts. Jesus has been powerless to prevent murder. The last shot is of a snow-covered cross with women's scalps hanging from it and blowing fiercely in the wind.

L'Age d'Or was shown in Paris for some months, until, one evening, a gang of Fascists staged a riot in the cinema.

After throwing stink-bombs, flinging purple ink at the screen and slashing the furnishings and Surrealist pictures in the foyer, the mob disappeared. The performance resumed. Sade's disturbing images, adapted by Buñuel, struck at the most reactionary forces on the Right in France.

And, in that sense, Sade's fantasies were mobilized in the cause of anti-Fascism.

An alternative cinematic political reading was advanced by Pier Paolo Pasolini (1922–75), Italian poet, novelist and extraordinary film-maker. He saw the fantasies produced by Sade in the light of horrors which, in our own day, have been acted out in the prisons, torture chambers and concentration camps of tyrannies all over the world. Pasolini made a film based on **The 120 Days**, called **Salò**, after the little North Italian town where Mussolini was installed as a puppet ruler by the Germans in 1943.

In the opening sequence of the film, we see the inmates on their way to the castle. Above their heads is a signpost that says Marzabotto, the name of a village where in 1944 the SS massacred 2,000 men, women and children. For Pasolini, the Château of Silling was a metaphor for Fascist tyranny. Is such a retrospective projection possible or valid? How do we square it with the Fascist riot in Paris in the 1930s?

"Should We Burn Sade?"

This is the title of a 1955 book on Sade by Simone de Beauvoir, just before a Paris law-court decision to seize and destroy four major published works of Sade.

Are the fantasies of **The 120 Days** to be deplored and censored because they might invite imitation? Or is it not the truth that human beings need no prompting to indulge in obscene rape, torture and killing?

Ian Brady and Myra Hindley, perpetrators of the infamous Moors Murders, said they found inspiration in Sade; but neither they nor the Nazi executioners needed to read Sade to carry out their crimes.

Mechanical Sade

The truth is that Sade is not an easy read. He is immensely repetitive, a tedious philosophical expounder and a mechanic of sexual excesses, tortures and killings.

The question is why was he banned for so long? Is he merely a "vile pornographer", as the radical feminist Andrea Dworkin calls him, the exemplar of misogyny and rape? Or can we judge the value of his "sadistic episodes" as daring and perilous explorations of the very darkest male fantasies in which extreme perversions of normal sexual behaviour find expression? That would be to give them a certain clinical value, and this is how Sade himself saw his "eccentricities". These tableaux, he writes, "help towards the development of the human spirit; our backwardness in this branch of learning may well be due to the restraint of those who venture to write upon such matters. Inhibited by absurd fears, they only discuss the puerilities with which every fool is familiar and dare not, by addressing themselves to the investigation of the human heart, offer its gigantic idiosyncracies to our view."

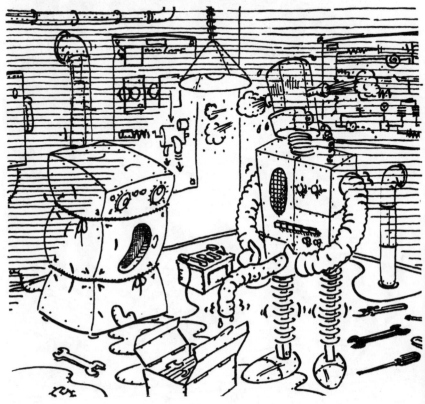

In the field of sexual behaviour, Sade had the courage to raise questions which are still being debated and apply to them a remorseless logic. He dealt with abortion and the point at which a foetus can be said to have "a soul"; with what constitutes "natural behaviour", which some people would limit by convention or by law (anal intercourse is illegal in certain American states); with what right the law has to interfere in sexual behaviour between consenting adults (as it did in the recent case of the gay men sentenced for sado-masochistic practices between consenting adults); about whether our sexuality is inborn or acquired; about the nature of marriage and the relationship of children to their parents.

Kafkaesque Sade

What remains deeply problematical is Sade's view that in sexual matters "might is right", an attitude which claims that the defenceless must submit to the desires of "aristocratic" men. This is the same attitude today of male tourist exploiters of child prostitutes in South-East Asia and South America, the ready-made script of snuff movies. And this is the criminal aspect of Sade's writing for which it is impossible not to condemn him.

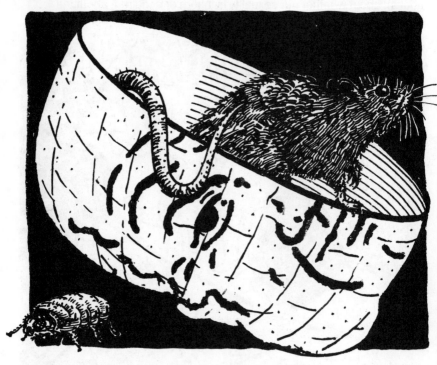

One gets the feeling from Sade that he is indeed a prisoner, physically and psychologically. His mind and spirit are entrapped as much as he himself was in his various prisons. He pursues a line of thought obsessively, pushing logic to the limits, drawing back from no conclusion, however terrible, as in his argument about the "naturalness" of murder. But he is caught in a circular argument from which there is no way out, just as there was for years apparently no way out of his places of detention. He was a prisoner of his circumstances and of his class and, to quote another materialist thinker, "if the circumstance in which the individual lives allows him only the one-sided development of a single quality at the expense of all the rest, then this individual achieves only a one-sided, crippled development." That was Sade's fate.

Judgement Reserved

That he was unjustly and harshly treated by men who, if comparisons were made, might not, as he wrote, "prove the winners in that parallel", is undoubtedly true. It is also true that he was courageous and unbroken. We have to admire his courage and determination, his intellectual daring, but there is a reservation to be made, which Simone de Beauvoir expressed in these terms: "To sympathize too readily with de Sade is to betray him . . . and every time we side with a child whose throat has been slit by a sex maniac we take a stand against him." But she goes on, "His merit lies in the fact that he did not simply resign himself . . . that he disputed all the easy answers . . . The supreme value of his testimony lies in his ability to disturb us."

Further Reading

The chief works of the Marquis de Sade are available in three volumes: **The One Hundred and Twenty Days of Sodom** (London, 1990), contains – besides his three-act play **Oxtiern or the Misfortunes of Libertinage** – an important essay by Simone de Beauvoir, "Must We Burn de Sade?" which discusses the moral questions posed by the man and his writings. **Justine** (London, 1991) also contains **The Dialogue between a Priest and a Dying Man** (a succinct statement of Sade's atheism), **Philosophy in the Bedroom**, which incudes his views not only on sexual relations but also on politics and society, and his **Last Will and Testament**. There are introductory essays by two distinguished French writers, Jean Paulhan and Maurice Blanchot. **Juliette** (1991) is Sade's longest and most sustained novel.

Most of the critical writing on Sade comes from France where he has long been considered a major literary and philosophical figure. Roland Barthes, **Sade/Fourier/Loyola** (New York, 1976) contains a brief perceptive account of the Marquis and his work. For an account of the influence of "the divine Marquis" in France and in Britain in the 19th century, see Mario Praz, **The Romantic Agony** (London, 1960). For his influence on the Surrealist movement, see André Breton, **What is Surrealism?** (1978) or Maurice Nadeau, **History of Surrealism** (London, 1978).

Geoffrey Gorer, **The Life and Ideas of the Marquis de Sade** (London, 1953) by the American sociologist is a good introduction. The most recent and highly documented life containing much new material is by Maurice Lever, **Marquis de Sade, A Biography** (London, 1993).

Three writers have produced studies of the subject in the light of feminist thinking and the debate on pornography. They are Angela Carter, **The Sadeian Woman** (London, 1979); Margaret Crossland, **The Passionate Philosopher** (London, 1991); Annie Le Brun, **Sade, A Sudden Abyss** (San Francisco, 1990).

Stuart Hood is a distinguished writer, translator, broadcaster and lecturer on the media. He has written of his experiences as a member of the Italian Resistance in World War II. He is also the author of **Fascism for Beginners** and co-author with Haim Bresheeth of **The Holocaust for Beginners**.

Graham Crowley was born in Romford, Essex in 1950. He studied painting at St Martin's School of Art, London and at the Royal College of Art. In 1982–83 he was the artist in residence to Oxford University. He has exhibited in Europe, America, Asia and Australia. He is currently Professor of Painting at the Royal College of Art.

A very special thank you to Sally for all her hard work.

Index